Happy Christmas
baby!
I've marked all
the soups I want
you to make
with a ☺!

Lots of love

Seb
Ⓧ

the BIG BOOK OF SOUPS

THE AUSTRALIAN **Women's Weekly**

the
BIG
BOOK OF
SOUPS

BAUER

CONTENTS

SATISFYING SOUPS

Since Neolithic times, soup has been known to possess restorative and nourishing qualities – the elderly and infirm were kept alive by being fed simple meat broths. This concept may have developed over the ages, but the premise remains the same: each of us can remember our mother perched on the edge of our sickbed, holding a bowl of chicken broth and urging us to eat because "it'll make you feel better".

Soup can be quickly made from a few inexpensive ingredients, and recent studies show that starting a meal with a low-fat soup can help with weight loss by decreasing the appetite for the following courses.

Soups form a staple food group in any cuisine, and are all improved if based on homemade stock (see recipes on pages 10-11). But for the convenience, ease and speed of preparation, the use of packaged stocks and demi-glaces, stock cubes and powder can't be denied. Use the best-quality prepared stock bases you can find, but bear in mind that these types of stock bases can be very salty or high in kilojoules.

TIPS FOR TOP SOUPS

DON'T OVERSEASON
When the soup is almost ready, test it for taste and, only then, add any necessary salt, pepper or other seasoning.

BUTTERMILK TASTES GREAT AND IS LOW-FAT
so it's good to use when making a cream soup. Pureed soup vegetables also can replace a portion of the cream or butter called for in the recipe. Low-fat evaporated milk can be used instead of some of the cream required in the recipe.

DON'T OVERCOOK OR FREEZE SOUPS
that contain rice, pasta or potatoes; add these ingredients just before serving so their texture remains slightly firm.

THICKENING SOUPS

The first, and most obvious way to thicken soup is simply to simmer it, uncovered, until some of the liquid evaporates and it cooks down to the desired thickness.

Puree some of the soup's solids (for instance, half the beans or peas, or some of the potato and carrot) then return the puree to the pan to thicken the broth.

Spoon a little of the hot broth into a small bowl, cool it for 5 minutes, then whisk a few tablespoons of plain flour into it until smooth. Stir it into the simmering soup. Cornflour or arrowroot can also be blended with a little cold water; stir this into simmering soup.

Grate a raw potato into the simmering soup; stir until cooked and the liquid has thickened.

Cream, yoghurt, sour cream, crème fraîche and even grated cheese can be used to thicken soups that will tolerate the addition of dairy products. It is advisable to stabilise the dairy product you're using by blending it with a little cornflour then whisking some of the hot stock into the cornflour mixture. Stir this mixture into the simmering soup.

DEFROST ANY STOCKS THAT ARE MEAT-BASED in the refrigerator and always bring them to the boil before finishing off the soup.

SOME FROZEN SOUPS need to be diluted and/or re-tasted for seasoning after they have thawed.

SMALL CUBES OF TOFU can be stirred into almost-finished vegetable soups for some added protein. Tofu has a neutral taste, so it readily absorbs the flavour of the soup.

VARIOUS HERBS AND VEGETABLES have particular qualities that they impart to soup, so it is best to consider them before using. For instance, celery leaves clouds a stock; carrots will darken and sweeten a broth; and the stalks of parsley, and some onions, can add a bitter flavour to stock.

HOMEMADE STOCK

Any of our basic stock recipes (pages 10-11) can take on Mediterranean or Asian undertones with a bit of ingenuity. Add fresh herbs shortly before the stock is finished, and dry-fry spices, separately, until they are just fragrant, before adding to the basic stock ingredients at the start of preparation.

CHOPPED CHILLI, fish sauce, kaffir lime leaves and lemon grass highlight the tastes of Thailand.

FRESH OREGANO or basil leaves, torn into pieces, and crushed garlic cloves convert stock into an Italian soup base (try adding a tablespoon of pesto as an alternative).

PRESERVED LEMON, CUMIN, CINNAMON and a teaspoon of harissa paste are reminiscent of Moroccan dishes.

LOTS OF CHOPPED PARSLEY, some olive oil, lemon juice and a dash of allspice brings the taste of Lebanon to your stockpot.

CLARIFY STOCK by stirring 1 lightly beaten egg white and 1 cracked egg shell per litre of stock into a pot of fairly cool stock. Return pot to a low heat; then slowly return stock to a simmer, without stirring. Simmer stock for 15 minutes, ignoring the frothy scum that appears on the surface. Take the stockpot off the heat and cool for about 30 minutes. Using a ladle, push the scum aside; scoop the stock into a muslin-lined sieve placed over a large bowl. Refrigerate until you're ready to freeze or use the stock.

BEFORE FREEZING STOCK, refrigerate it until it's cold. Any fat in the stock rises to form a solid surface; carefully scoop this fat off the top of the stock and discard it. If you like, instead of discarding the fat, use it to fry any meat or vegetables being used in the dish.

IF YOU WANT TO USE STOCK STRAIGHTAWAY, and have no time to set the fat, try blotting the surface of the soup gently with a few sheets of absorbent kitchen paper.

FREEZE THE COOLED STOCK in quantities to suit your needs. It can be frozen in empty, cleaned 300ml, 600ml or 1 litre milk cartons; fill to about 3cm from the top of the container, cover with a small plastic bag and stand upright in the freezer until frozen. The stock will expand as it freezes, so the gap left at the top and the looseness of the plastic bag allow for this. Once frozen, seal the stock in the carton using masking tape or rubber bands; stack the cartons on their sides in the freezer. You can also freeze stock in ice-cube trays; once frozen, place the cubes in a ziptop plastic bag and use singly or as required.

GARNISHES serve a practical, as well as an aesthetic purpose: shavings of pumpkin or carrot help to identify orange-coloured soups; finely chopped chilli and coriander leaves turn a simple tomato broth into a Mexican delight; and sour cream and chopped chives are necessities for borscht.

FOR THICK SOUPS, garnish with: slices of cucumber, lemon, onion or tomato; slices of toasted french bread topped with melted cheese; delicious dumplings; whole roasted tiny vegetables or ravioli.

FOR SMOOTH OR CREAM SOUPS, garnish with: coarsely chopped or tiny whole leaves of (micro) herbs; contrasting coloured pureed vegetables or crème fraîche swirled into the surface; lightly fried shredded green onion or slices of garlic or flavoured fried croûtons.

FOR BROTHS OR CONSOMMES, garnish with: finely shredded lemon rind; thinly sliced green herbs; a few crunchy fried noodles or tiny shards of toasted pitta or tortilla; thin strands of finely shredded carrot, cucumber, daikon or red onion.

STOCKS

These recipes can be made up to 4 days ahead, and kept, covered, in the fridge, or frozen for up to 3 months.

BEEF

Preheat oven to 200°C/350°F. Roast 2kg (4 pounds) meaty beef bones on an oven tray for 1 hour or until browned. Combine bones and 2 coarsely chopped medium brown onions with 5½ litres (22 cups) water, 2 coarsely chopped trimmed celery stalks, 2 coarsely chopped medium carrots, 2 teaspoons black peppercorns and 3 fresh bay leaves in a large saucepan or boiler; bring to the boil, then simmer, uncovered, for 3 hours, skimming the surface occasionally. Add 3 litres (12 cups) extra water; simmer, uncovered, for 1 hour. Strain stock through a muslin-lined sieve or colander into a large heatproof bowl; discard solids. Allow stock to cool, cover; refrigerate until cold. Skim and discard surface fat before using.

prep + cook time 5¼ hours (+ cooling & refrigeration) **makes** 3.5 litres (14 cups)

nutritional count per 1 cup (250ml)
2g total fat (0.9g saturated fat); 259kJ (62 cal); 2.3g carbohydrate; 8g protein; 1.1g fibre

CHICKEN

Combine 2kg (4 pounds) chicken bones, 2 coarsely chopped medium brown onions, 2 coarsely chopped trimmed celery stalks, 2 coarsely chopped medium carrots, 3 fresh bay leaves, 2 teaspoons black peppercorns and 5 litres (20 cups) water in a large saucepan or boiler; simmer, uncovered, for 2 hours, skimming the surface occasionally. Strain stock through a muslin-lined sieve or colander into a large heatproof bowl; discard solids. Allow stock to cool, cover; refrigerate until cold. Skim and discard surface fat before using.

prep + cook time 2¼ hours (+ cooling & refrigeration) **makes** 3.5 litres (14 cups)

nutritional count per 1 cup (250ml)
0.6g total fat (0.2g saturated fat); 105kJ (25 cal); 2.3g carbohydrate; 1.9g protein; 1.1g fibre

VEGETABLE

Place 4 coarsely chopped medium brown onions, 2 coarsely chopped large carrots, 10 coarsely chopped trimmed celery stalks, 2 coarsely chopped large parsnips, 6 litres (24 cups) water, 4 fresh bay leaves and 2 teaspoons black peppercorns in a large saucepan; simmer, uncovered, for 1½ hours. Strain stock through a muslin-lined sieve or colander into a large heatproof bowl; discard solids. Allow stock to cool. Cover; refrigerate until cold. Skim and discard surface fat before using.

FISH

Place 1.5kg (3 pounds) fish bones, 3 litres (12 cups) water, 1 coarsely chopped medium white onion, 2 trimmed coarsely chopped stalks celery, 2 fresh bay leaves and 1 teaspoon black peppercorns in a large saucepan; simmer, uncovered, for 20 minutes. Strain stock through a muslin-lined sieve or colander into a large heatproof bowl; discard solids. Allow stock to cool. Cover; refrigerate until cold. Skim and discard surface fat before using.

---

prep + cook time 1¾ hours (+ cooling & refrigeration) **makes** 3.5 litres (14 cups)

nutritional count per 1 cup (250ml)
0.2g total fat (0g saturated fat); 151kJ (36 cal); 5.7g carbohydrate; 1.4g protein; 2.9g fibre

---

prep + cook time 25 minutes (+ cooling & refrigeration) **makes** 2.5 litres (10 cups)

nutritional count per 1 cup (250ml)
0.2g total fat (0.1g saturated fat); 63kJ (15 cal); 1.1g carbohydrate; 1.9g protein; 0.6g fibre

---

11

SEAFOOD

SEAFOOD LAKSA

prep + cook time 1¼ hours **serves** 6

12 uncooked medium king prawns (shrimp)
   (540g)
1 litre (4 cups) chicken stock
800ml coconut milk
4 fresh kaffir lime leaves, shredded finely
150g (4½ ounces) rice stick noodles
300g (9½ ounces) scallops, roe removed
150g (4½ ounces) marinated tofu,
   cut into 2cm (¾-inch) pieces
2 tablespoons lime juice
2 cups (160g) bean sprouts
4 green onions (scallions), sliced thinly
1 fresh long red chilli, sliced thinly
½ cup loosely packed fresh coriander leaves
   (cilantro)

LAKSA PASTE
3 medium dried chillies
⅓ cup (80ml) boiling water
2 teaspoons peanut oil
1 small brown onion (80g), chopped coarsely
2 cloves garlic, quartered
2cm (¾-inch) piece fresh ginger (10g), grated
10cm (4-inch) stick fresh lemon grass (20g),
   chopped finely
1 tablespoon halved unroasted, unsalted
   macadamias
1 tablespoon coarsely chopped fresh
   coriander (cilantro) root and stem mixture
½ teaspoon each ground turmeric and
   coriander
¼ cup loosely packed fresh mint leaves

1 Shell and devein prawns, leaving tails intact.
2 Make laksa paste.
3 Cook paste in a large saucepan over medium heat, stirring, about 5 minutes or until fragrant. Stir in stock, coconut milk and lime leaves; bring to the boil. Reduce heat; simmer, covered, 20 minutes.
4 Meanwhile, place noodles in a large heatproof bowl, cover with boiling water; stand until tender, drain.
5 Add prawns to laksa mixture; simmer, uncovered, about 5 minutes or until prawns change in colour. Add scallops and tofu; simmer, uncovered, about 3 minutes or until scallops change in colour. Remove from heat; stir in juice, season to taste.
6 Divide noodles among serving bowls; ladle laksa into bowls, top with sprouts, onion, chilli and coriander.

LAKSA PASTE Cover chillies with the boiling water in a small heatproof bowl; stand for 10 minutes, drain. Blend or process chillies with remaining ingredients until smooth.

---

nutritional count per serving 35.4g total fat (25.9g saturated fat); 2207kJ (528 cal); 25.1g carbohydrate; 25.7g protein; 5g fibre

notes Recipe is not suitable to freeze. Various-flavoured marinated tofu can be found in the refrigerated section in larger supermarkets.

HOT & SOUR PRAWN NOODLE SOUP

prep + cook time 25 minutes **serves** 4

1½ cups (375ml) fish stock

1.5 litres (6 cups) water

3 fresh kaffir lime leaves, torn in half

10cm (4-inch) stick fresh lemon grass (20g), halved lengthways

3cm (1¼-inch) piece fresh ginger (15g), sliced thinly

⅓ cup (75g) tom yum paste

2 tablespoons fish sauce

½ cup (125ml) lime juice

⅓ cup (75g) firmly packed brown sugar

200g (6½ ounces) dried rice stick noodles

400g (12½ ounces) baby buk choy, quartered

200g (6½ ounces) button mushrooms, halved

400g (12½ ounces) uncooked shelled medium king prawns (shrimp)

3 fresh small red thai (serrano) chillies, sliced thinly

¼ cup loosely packed fresh coriander (cilantro) leaves

1 Place stock, the water, lime leaves, lemon grass and ginger in a large saucepan; bring to the boil. Reduce heat; simmer, covered, 5 minutes. Remove lime leaves, lemon grass and ginger with a slotted spoon. Stir in paste; return to the boil. Stir in the sauce, juice and sugar.

2 Meanwhile, place noodles in a large heatproof bowl; cover with boiling water, stand for 5 minutes or until tender. Drain.

3 Add buk choy to the stock mixture with mushrooms, prawns and chilli; simmer, uncovered, until prawns change colour. Stir in noodles; simmer, uncovered, until hot. Season to taste.

4 Serve soup with coriander, and a squeeze of lime, if you like.

nutritional count per serving 3.2g total fat (0.5g saturated fat); 1201kJ (287 cal); 32.9g carbohydrate; 28.2g protein; 5.4g fibre

notes Recipe is not suitable to freeze. Shelled prawns are available in seafood shops and frozen in supermarkets.

NEW ENGLAND CLAM CHOWDER

prep + cook time 40 minutes (+ standing) **serves** 4

1kg (2 pounds) baby clams
2 tablespoons coarse cooking salt
  (kosher salt)
40g (1½ ounces) butter
1 large brown onion (200g),
  chopped coarsely
2 rindless bacon slices (130g),
  chopped coarsely
1 clove garlic, crushed
2 tablespoons plain (all-purpose) flour
3 cups (750ml) milk, warmed
2 cups (500ml) vegetable stock, warmed
2 medium potatoes (400g), chopped coarsely
2 tablespoons coarsely chopped fresh chives

1 Rinse clams under cold water; place in a large bowl; sprinkle with salt, cover with water. Stand 1 hour; rinse, drain.

2 Melt butter in a large saucepan over medium heat; add onion, bacon and garlic to pan. Cook, stirring, until onion softens. Add flour; cook, stirring, until mixture thickens and bubbles. Gradually stir in warmed milk and stock; stir until mixture boils and thickens slightly. Add potato, reduce heat; simmer, covered, until potato is tender.

3 Add clams; simmer, covered, for 5 minutes or until clams open. Remove from heat; stir in chives, season to taste. Serve chowder with grilled slices of french bread.

nutritional count per serving 19.4g total fat (8.8g saturated fat); 1672kJ (400 cal); 28.7g carbohydrate; 26.4g protein; 2.5g fibre

notes Recipe is not suitable to freeze. If clams aren't available, replace them with pipis. Fish stock can be used instead of vegetable stock.

TOM YUM GOONG

prep + cook time 50 minutes serves 4

1.5 litres (6 cups) fish stock

1 tablespoon coarsely chopped coriander
(cilantro) root and stem mixture

10cm (4-inch) stick fresh lemon grass (20g),
sliced thinly

8 kaffir lime leaves, torn

8cm (3¼-inch) piece fresh ginger (40g),
sliced thinly

2 fresh small red thai (serrano) chillies,
sliced thinly

1 tablespoon fish sauce

12 uncooked large king prawns (shrimp)
(840g)

8 green onions (scallions), cut into
2cm (¾-inch) lengths

⅓ cup (80ml) lime juice

⅔ cup coarsely chopped fresh coriander
(cilantro)

½ cup loosely packed fresh thai basil leaves,
torn roughly

1 Place stock, coriander root and stem
mixture, lemon grass, lime leaves, ginger,
chilli and sauce in a large saucepan; bring
to the boil. Reduce heat; simmer, uncovered,
10 minutes.

2 Meanwhile, shell and devein prawns, leaving
tails intact.

3 Add prawns, onion and juice to pan; simmer,
uncovered, about 4 minutes or until prawns
change colour. Remove from heat; stir in
chopped coriander and basil leaves, season.

nutritional count per serving 1.6g total fat
(0.5g saturated fat); 602kJ (114 cal);
4.4g carbohydrate; 27g protein; 1.4g fibre

notes Recipe is not suitable to freeze.
Wash the coriander stems and roots well, then
chop the required amount for this recipe.

CREAMY CRAB & TOMATO BISQUE

prep + cook time 1¾ hours **serves** 4

4 uncooked medium blue swimmer crabs
  (1.3kg)
60g (2 ounces) butter
1 medium brown onion (150g),
  chopped coarsely
1 medium carrot (120g), chopped coarsely
1 medium leek (350g), chopped coarsely
2 cloves garlic, crushed
1 tablespoon tomato paste
2 tablespoons brandy
1 cup (250ml) dry white wine
1.25 litres (5 cups) fish stock
1 bay leaf
2 sprigs fresh thyme
2 medium tomatoes (300g), chopped finely
20g (¾ ounces) butter, extra
1 tablespoon plain (all-purpose) flour
½ cup (125ml) pouring cream

1 Slide knife under top of crab shells at back, lever off and discard. Discard gills; rinse crabs under cold water. Using a cleaver or heavy knife, chop each body into quarters.
2 Melt butter in a large saucepan over medium heat; cook onion, carrot, leek and garlic, stirring, until vegetables soften. Add crab, in batches; cook, stirring, until changed in colour. Remove from pan.
3 Add paste to pan; cook, stirring, 2 minutes. Return crab to pan with brandy; stir over heat for 2 minutes or until alcohol evaporates.
4 Add wine, stock, bay leaf, thyme and tomato; bring to the boil. Reduce heat; simmer, uncovered, for 45 minutes.
5 Meanwhile, using the back of a teaspoon, work extra butter into flour in a small bowl.
6 Strain soup through a muslin-lined sieve or colander into a large heatproof bowl; extract as much meat as possible from crab, add to soup. Discard shells, claws and other solids.
7 Return soup to pan; bring to the boil. Stir in flour mixture and cream; stir until soup boils and thickens slightly. Season to taste.

nutritional count per serving 32g total fat (20.1g saturated fat); 2152kJ (515 cal); 13.1g carbohydrate; 27.1g protein; 4.4g fibre

notes Recipe is not suitable to freeze. Making your own fish stock will enhance the flavour of this dish – see page 11 for the recipe.

BOUILLABAISSE

prep + cook time 1½ hours serves 6

You need an extra large saucepan to fit in all the seafood.

6 uncooked small blue swimmer crabs (2kg)
2 tablespoons olive oil
4 cloves garlic, crushed
2 medium white onions (300g), chopped finely
¼ cup (70g) tomato paste
¾ cup (180ml) dry white wine
800g (1½ pounds) canned chopped tomatoes
½ teaspoon ground turmeric
2 bay leaves
2 teaspoons white (granulated) sugar
1½ cups (375ml) water
1kg (2 pounds) firm white fish fillets, chopped coarsely
500g (1 pound) uncooked large king prawns (shrimp)
250g (8 ounces) scallops, roe removed
250g (8 ounces) calamari rings

1 Slide knife under top of crab shells at back, lever off and discard. Discard gills; rinse crabs under cold water. Crack nippers slightly; using a cleaver or heavy knife, chop each body in half.
2 Heat oil in a large saucepan over medium heat; cook garlic and onion, stirring, until onion is soft. Stir in tomato paste, wine, tomatoes, turmeric, bay leaves, sugar and the water; bring to the boil. Reduce heat; simmer, uncovered, for 10 minutes.
3 Add crab and fish to tomato mixture; bring to the boil. Reduce heat; simmer, covered, for 5 minutes.
4 Meanwhile, shell and devein prawns leaving tails intact.
5 Stir prawns, scallops and calamari into tomato mixture; bring to the boil. Reduce heat; simmer, uncovered, until prawns change colour. Season to taste.
6 Serve bouillabaisse immediately, with fresh crusty bread, if desired.

nutritional count per serving 11.7g total fat (2.4g saturated fat); 1843kJ (441 cal); 11.3g carbohydrate; 67.2g protein; 3.1g fibre

notes Recipe not suitable to freeze. Recipe must be made and served immediately as seafood does not reheat successfully.

SEAFOOD CHOWDER

prep + cook time 50 minutes **serves** 6

1 tablespoon olive oil
3 rindless bacon slices (195g), sliced thinly
1 medium brown onion (150g),
  chopped finely
1 small fennel bulb (200g), sliced thinly
3 cloves garlic, sliced thinly
2 medium tomatoes (300g), seeded,
  chopped coarsely
2 tablespoons tomato paste
1 teaspoon hot paprika
½ cup (125ml) dry white wine
800g (1½ pounds) canned whole tomatoes
3 cups (750ml) fish stock
1 litre (4 cups) water
500g (1 pound) kipfler potatoes, cut into
  2.5cm (1-inch) pieces
1.2kg (2½ pounds) marinara mix
½ cup coarsely chopped fresh
  flat-leaf parsley

1 Heat oil in a large saucepan over medium heat; cook bacon, stirring, until crisp. Drain on absorbent paper.

2 Add onion, fennel and garlic to pan; cook, stirring, until vegetables soften. Add chopped tomato; cook, stirring, until soft. Add tomato paste and paprika; cook for 2 minutes. Return bacon to pan with wine; cook, stirring, for 2 minutes.

3 Slice canned tomatoes thickly; add slices with juice from can, stock, the water and potato to pan; bring to the boil. Reduce heat; simmer, covered, about 20 minutes or until potato is soft.

4 Add marinara mix; cook, covered, for 3 minutes until seafood is just cooked. Stir in parsley; season to taste.

nutritional count per serving 8.8g total fat (2.2g saturated fat); 1781kJ (426 cal); 24.5g carbohydrate; 50.5g protein; 5.7g fibre

notes Recipe is not suitable to freeze. Marinara mix is a mixture of chopped raw seafood available from the supermarket seafood section.

FISH CHOWDER

prep + cook time 40 minutes **serves** 4

40g (1½ ounces) butter

1 large brown onion (200g), chopped coarsely

1 clove garlic, crushed

2 rindless bacon slices (130g),
  chopped coarsely

2 tablespoons plain (all-purpose) flour

2 medium potatoes (400g), chopped coarsely

3 cups (750ml) milk

2 cups (500ml) vegetable stock

400g (12½ ounces) firm white fish fillets,
  chopped coarsely

2 tablespoons finely chopped fresh chives

1 Melt butter in a large saucepan over medium heat; cook onion, garlic and bacon, stirring, 5 minutes or until onion softens.

2 Add flour; cook, stirring, 1 minute. Add potato, milk and stock; bring to the boil. Reduce heat; simmer, covered, about 10 minutes or until potato is tender.

3 Add fish; simmer, uncovered, about 4 minutes or until fish is cooked through. Serve soup sprinkled with chives; accompany with crusty wholemeal bread, if you like.

nutritional count per serving 19.5g total fat (11.6g saturated fat); 1810kJ (433 cal); 28.4g carbohydrate; 34.8g protein; 2.4g fibre

notes Recipe is not suitable to freeze. Use any firm white fish fillets, such as perch, ling or blue-eye trevalla, for this recipe.

ITALIAN SEAFOOD SOUP

prep + cook time 1¼ hours **serves** 4

1 tablespoon olive oil

1 medium brown onion (150g), chopped finely

3 cloves garlic, crushed

700g (1½ pounds) bottled tomato pasta sauce (passata)

1½ cups (375ml) fish stock

½ cup (125ml) dry white wine

2 strips lemon rind

600g (1¼ pounds) uncooked medium king prawns (shrimp)

600g (1¼ pounds) firm white fish fillets

300g (9½ ounces) clams, scrubbed

12 scallops without roe (300g)

¼ cup finely shredded fresh basil

¼ cup coarsely chopped fresh flat-leaf parsley

1 Heat oil in a large saucepan over medium heat; cook onion and garlic, stirring, for 5 minutes or until onion softens. Add passata, stock, wine and rind; bring to the boil. Reduce heat; simmer, covered, 20 minutes.

2 Meanwhile, shell and devein prawns, leaving tails intact. Cut fish into 2cm (¾-inch) pieces.

3 Add clams to pan; cook, covered, for 5 minutes. Add prawns, fish and scallops to pan; cook, covered, stirring occasionally, 5 minutes or until seafood just changes colour. Stir in herbs; season to taste.

nutritional count per serving 9.4g total fat (2g saturated fat); 1772kJ (424 cal); 14.5g carbohydrate; 62g protein; 4.7g fibre

notes Recipe is not suitable to freeze. Use the same amount of marinara mix in place of the seafood, if you prefer.

SPICY SEAFOOD SOUP

prep + cook time 50 minutes **serves** 4

1 uncooked medium blue swimmer crab (500g)

150g (4½ ounces) firm white fish fillets

8 medium black mussels (200g)

150g (4½ ounces) cleaned squid hoods

1.25 litres (5 cups) chicken stock

2 x 10cm (4-inch) sticks fresh lemon grass (40g), chopped finely

4cm (1½-inch) piece fresh galangal (20g), sliced thinly

4 fresh kaffir lime leaves

6 fresh small green thai chillies, chopped coarsely

4 dried long red chillies, chopped finely

8 uncooked large prawns (shrimp) (400g)

1 teaspoon grated palm sugar

2 tablespoons fish sauce

1 tablespoon lime juice

¼ cup loosely packed fresh thai basil leaves

1 Slide knife under top of crab shell at back, lever off and discard. Discard gills; rinse crab under cold water. Using a cleaver or heavy knife, chop the body into quarters, leaving claws intact.

2 Cut fish into bite-sized portions; scrub mussels, remove beards. Cut squid into 2cm (¾-inch) thick slices; score the inside in a diagonal pattern.

3 Place stock, lemon grass, galangal, lime leaves and both chillies in a large saucepan; bring to the boil.

4 Add prepared seafood and unshelled prawns to boiling stock mixture; cook, uncovered, about 5 minutes or until seafood is just cooked through and mussels open. Remove from heat; stir in remaining ingredients. Season to taste.

nutritional count per serving 3.4g total fat (1.2g saturated fat); 807kJ (193 cal); 6.1g carbohydrate; 33.9g protein; 0.9g fibre

notes Recipe is not suitable to freeze. Use any firm white fish fillets, such as perch, ling or blue-eye trevalla, for this recipe.

VIETNAMESE PRAWN SOUP

prep + cook time 55 minutes **serves** 6

500g (1 pound) uncooked medium king
  prawns (shrimps)
2cm (¾-inch) piece fresh ginger (10g),
  sliced thinly
1 teaspoon black peppercorns
2 cloves garlic, crushed
2 fresh long red chillies, sliced thinly
10cm (4-inch) stick fresh lemon grass
  (20g), sliced coarsely
3 litres (12 cups) water
400g (12½ ounces) fresh rice noodles
¼ cup (60ml) lemon juice
⅓ cup (80ml) fish sauce, approximately
2 green onions (scallions), sliced thinly
⅓ cup firmly packed fresh coriander leaves
  (cilantro)
¼ cup firmly packed fresh mint leaves

1 Peel and devein prawns, discard heads. Place prawn shells, ginger, peppercorns, garlic, half the chilli, lemon grass and the water in a large saucepan; bring to the boil. Reduce heat; simmer, uncovered, for 20 minutes. Strain stock; return liquid to same cleaned pan, discard solids.
2 Add prawns to stock; simmer, covered, for 3 minutes or until prawns change colour.
3 Meanwhile, place noodles in a large heatproof bowl; cover with boiling water. Separate noodles with a fork; drain.
4 Add juice to stock, gradually add fish sauce to taste. Divide prawns and noodles evenly among serving bowls; top with stock, onion, herbs and remaining chilli.

nutritional count per serving 0.7g total fat (0.1g saturated fat); 493kJ (118 cal); 15.8g carbohydrate; 11.3g protein; 1g fibre

notes Recipe is not suitable to freeze. Peel away the tough outer layers of the lemon grass and use the tender white part at the base.

CREAMY SCALLOP SOUP WITH CARAMELISED LEEK

prep + cook time 1 hour (+ cooling) **serves** 4

40g (1½ ounces) butter
4 shallots (100g), chopped finely
2 cloves garlic, crushed
3 cups (750ml) water
3 cups (750ml) fish stock
¼ cup (60ml) dry white wine
2 medium potatoes (400g), chopped coarsely
1 tablespoon plain (all-purpose) flour
½ cup (125ml) pouring cream
350g (11 ounces) scallops, roe removed
1 tablespoon finely chopped fresh chives

CARAMELISED LEEK

20g (¾ ounce) butter
1 large leek (500g), sliced thinly
1 tablespoon white (granulated) sugar
¼ cup (60ml) dry white wine

1 Melt half the butter in a large saucepan over medium heat; cook shallot and garlic, stirring, until softened. Add the water, stock, wine and potato; bring to the boil. Reduce heat; simmer, uncovered, about 15 minutes or until potato is tender. Remove from heat, cool 15 minutes.
2 Meanwhile, make caramelised leek.
3 Using the back of a teaspoon, work the remaining butter into flour in a small bowl.
4 Blend or process soup, in batches, until smooth. Return soup to pan; add flour mixture. Return to the boil, stirring, then remove from heat. Stir in cream and scallops; stand, covered, 3 minutes. Season to taste.
5 Serve soup sprinkled with leek and chives.

CARAMELISED LEEK Melt butter in a medium saucepan over medium heat; cook leek, stirring, about 5 minutes or until softened. Add sugar and wine, reduce heat to low; cook, stirring, about 15 minutes or until leek is caramelised.

nutritional count per serving 27.3g total fat (17.4g saturated fat); 1827kJ (437 cal); 24.2g carbohydrate; 17.3g protein; 4.1g fibre

notes Recipe is not suitable to freeze. Use a potato variety that holds its shape during boiling: desiree, nicola or pontiac are all good.

SEAFOOD TIPS

HOW CAN YOU TELL IF SEAFOOD IS FRESH?

FRESH SEAFOOD WILL HAVE A LIGHT, FRESH 'SEA' SMELL; ANY SEAFOOD THAT SMELLS 'FISHY' IS NOT GOOD TO EAT. FISH SHOULD HAVE A FIRM, MOIST

FLESH AND BRIGHT EYES. CRUSTACEANS WILL HAVE BRIGHTLY COLOURED SHELLS AND FLESH, AND MOLLUSCS SHOULD BE CLOSED, WITH NO DISCOLOURATION AT THE JOINTS.

MUSSELS IN SPICED COCONUT BROTH

prep + cook time 45 minutes serves 4

1kg (2 pounds) medium black mussels
1 cup (250ml) water
3 cups (750ml) fish stock
10cm (4-inch) piece fresh ginger (50g),
   sliced thinly
2 fresh small red thai (serrano) chillies,
   sliced thinly
4 cloves garlic, sliced thinly
3 dried curry leaves
4 shallots (100g), sliced thinly
1 tablespoon fish sauce
1 teaspoon finely grated lemon rind
2 teaspoons lemon juice
½ cup (125ml) coconut milk
1 cup firmly packed fresh coriander leaves
   (cilantro)

1 Scrub mussels; remove beards.
2 Place the water and stock in a large saucepan with ginger, chilli, garlic, curry leaves, shallot, sauce, rind, juice and coconut milk; bring to the boil. Reduce heat; simmer, covered, 20 minutes.
3 Add mussels; simmer, covered, about 5 minutes or until mussels open. Season to taste.
4 Serve soup sprinkled with coriander.

nutritional count per serving 8g total fat
(6.2g saturated fat); 585kJ (140 cal);
6.7g carbohydrate; 9.7g protein; 1.7g fibre

notes Recipe is not suitable to freeze.
Dried curry leaves keep indefinitely in an airtight container, but their flavour diminishes over time.

MEDITERRANEAN FISH SOUP

prep + cook time 1 hour **serves** 4

1 tablespoon olive oil

1 clove garlic, crushed

1 small leek (200g), halved, sliced thinly

1 small red capsicum (bell pepper) (150g),
cut into 1cm (½-inch) pieces

1 small red onion (100g), halved, sliced thinly

1 stalk celery (150g), trimmed, cut into
1cm (½-inch) pieces

1 small carrot (70g), cut into 1cm
(½-inch) pieces

½ teaspoon finely grated orange rind

¼ teaspoon dried chilli flakes

2 tablespoons tomato paste

2 cups (500ml) water

3 cups (750ml) fish stock

¼ cup (60ml) dry white wine

2 large egg (plum) tomatoes (180g),
chopped coarsely

200g (6½ ounces) uncooked small
king prawns (shrimp)

200g (6½ ounces) firm white fish fillets,
chopped coarsely

200g (6½ ounces) skinless ocean trout
fillet, chopped coarsely

¼ teaspoon finely chopped fresh thyme

1 tablespoon finely chopped fresh dill

1 Heat oil in a large saucepan over medium heat; cook garlic, leek, capsicum, onion, celery, carrot, rind and chilli, stirring, until vegetables soften.

2 Add paste, the water, stock, wine and tomato; bring to the boil. Reduce heat; simmer, uncovered, 20 minutes.

3 Meanwhile, shell and devein prawns; chop meat coarsely. Add prawn meat, fish, thyme and half the dill to soup; simmer, uncovered, about 3 minutes or until prawn and fish are cooked and changed in colour. Season to taste.

4 Serve soup sprinkled with remaining dill.

nutritional count per serving 7.7g total fat (1.4g saturated fat); 978kJ (234 cal); 8.5g carbohydrate; 28.3g protein; 3.7g fibre

notes Recipe is not suitable to freeze. Use any firm white fish fillets, such as perch, ling or blue-eye trevalla, for this recipe.

THAI SALMON BROTH WITH SESAME STICKY RICE PATTIES

prep + cook time 50 minutes (+ standing) **serves** 4

2 cups (500ml) water
3 cups (750ml) fish stock
3 x 10cm (4-inch) sticks fresh lemon grass
   (60g), bruised
3 fresh kaffir lime leaves, torn
1 fresh long red chilli, sliced thinly
2cm (¾-inch) piece fresh ginger (10g), grated
440g (14 ounces) skinless salmon fillets
1 tablespoon fish sauce
2 tablespoons lime juice
150g (4½ ounces) snow peas, trimmed,
   halved crossways
230g (7 ounces) can sliced bamboo shoots,
   rinsed, drained
3 green onions (scallions), sliced thinly

SESAME STICKY RICE PATTIES

1 cup (200g) glutinous rice
1 tablespoon toasted black sesame seeds
1½ tablespoons rice wine vinegar

1 Start making sesame sticky rice patties.
2 The next day, continue making sesame sticky rice patties.
3 Combine the water, stock, lemon grass, lime leaves, chilli and ginger in a large saucepan; bring to the boil. Reduce heat; simmer, uncovered, 10 minutes.
4 Add fish to pan; simmer, uncovered, for 10 minutes or until cooked as desired. Transfer fish to medium bowl; using fork, flake into small pieces.
5 Stir sauce, juice, snow peas and bamboo shoots into soup; simmer, uncovered, about 2 minutes or until snow peas are just tender. Discard lemon grass. Season to taste.
6 Divide fish and rice patties into bowls; ladle soup into bowls, sprinkle with onion.

SESAME STICKY RICE PATTIES Cover rice with water; stand overnight. The next day, drain rice; rinse well under cold water, drain. Place rice in a bamboo or metal steamer lined with muslin or cloth. Place steamer over a saucepan of boiling water, cover tightly; steam about 20 minutes or until rice is tender. Combine rice in a medium bowl with seeds and vinegar; roll level tablespoons of rice mixture into balls. Gently flatten balls, place on tray; cover with damp tea towel until required.

nutritional count per serving 10.3g total fat (2.2g saturated fat); 402kJ (176 cal); 44.7g carbohydrate; 30.4g protein; 2.9g fibre

note Recipe is not suitable to freeze. Asian supermarkets will stock glutinous rice; the grains of this 'sticky' rice clump together.

CHILLI CRAB LAKSA

prep + cook time 1½ hours (+ standing) **serves** 4

2 uncooked whole mud crabs (1.5kg)
2 tablespoons peanut oil
3 fresh long red chillies, chopped finely
2 cloves garlic, crushed
2cm (¾ inch) piece fresh ginger (10g), grated
½ cup (125ml) fish stock
⅔ cup (180g) laksa paste
800ml can coconut milk
1 litre (4 cups) chicken stock
3 fresh kaffir lime leaves, shredded finely
1 fresh long red chilli, chopped finely, extra
1 tablespoon lime juice
1 tablespoon fish sauce
1 tablespoon grated palm sugar
250g (8 ounces) dried rice stick noodles
3 green onions (scallions), sliced thinly
3 cups (240g) bean sprouts
½ cup loosely packed fresh coriander leaves
   (cilantro)

1 Place crabs in a large container filled with ice and water; stand 1 hour. Prepare crab by lifting tail flap and, with a peeling motion, lift off back shell. Remove and discard whitish gills, liver and brain matter. Leaving flesh in claws and legs, crack claws with the back of a heavy knife. Rinse crabs well. Using a cleaver or heavy knife, chop each body into quarters; crack large claws with the back of a knife.
2 Heat oil in a wok; stir-fry chilli, garlic and ginger until fragrant. Add crab and fish stock to wok; bring to the boil. Reduce heat; simmer, covered, about 20 minutes or until crab is changed in colour. Discard liquid in wok.
3 Meanwhile, cook paste in a large saucepan over medium heat, stirring, until fragrant. Stir in coconut milk, chicken stock, lime leaf and extra chilli; bring to the boil. Reduce heat; simmer, covered, 20 minutes. Stir in juice, sauce and sugar; season to taste.
4 Meanwhile, place noodles in a large heatproof bowl; cover with boiling water. Stand until tender; drain.
5 Divide noodles and crab among serving bowls; ladle laksa into bowls, top with onion, sprouts and coriander.

nutritional count per serving 68.2g total fat (40g saturated fat); 4088kJ (978 cal); 31.6g carbohydrate; 55.9g protein; 10.8g fibre

notes Recipe is not suitable to freeze. Some laksa pastes are very hot, so if you have a low heat tolerance, use less of the laksa paste.

CHUNKY FISH CHOWDER

prep + cook time 40 minutes **serves** 4

1 tablespoon olive oil

2 rindless shortcut bacon slices (60g), chopped coarsely

1 medium brown onion (150g), chopped finely

2 stalks celery (300g), trimmed, chopped finely

2 cloves garlic, crushed

1 tablespoon plain (all-purpose) flour

1 cup (250ml) milk, warmed

600g (1¼ pounds) kipfler potatoes, sliced thickly

2 cups (500ml) fish stock

1 cup (250ml) water

600g (1¼ pounds) white fish fillets, cut into 2.5cm (1-inch) pieces

½ cup coarsely chopped fresh flat-leaf parsley

1 teaspoon finely grated lemon rind

1 Heat oil in a large saucepan over medium heat; cook bacon, stirring, until crisp. Add onion, celery and garlic; cook, stirring, until onion is soft.

2 Add flour to pan; cook, stirring, until mixture bubbles and thickens. Gradually stir in warmed milk. Add potatoes, stock and the water; bring to the boil, stirring. Reduce heat; simmer, uncovered, about 10 minutes or until potato is tender.

3 Add fish to soup; cook, stirring occasionally, until fish is cooked. Remove from heat; stir in parsley and rind, season to taste.

nutritional count per serving 12.9g total fat (4.2g saturated fat); 1714kJ (410 cal); 28.4g carbohydrate; 42g protein; 5.1g fibre

notes Recipe is not suitable to freeze. We used flathead fillets in this recipe, but perch, ling or blue-eye trevalla are all fine.

PRAWN LAKSA

prep + cook time 1¼ hours serves 4

1 tablespoon vegetable oil
800ml can coconut milk
1 litre (4 cups) chicken stock
1 tablespoon brown sugar
2 teaspoons fish sauce
6 fresh kaffir lime leaves, shredded finely
1kg (2 pounds) uncooked medium
    king prawns (shrimp)
250g (8 ounces) fresh thin egg noodles
125g (4 ounces) dried thin rice noodles
1 cup (80g) bean sprouts
¼ cup loosely packed fresh coriander leaves
    (cilantro)
1 lime, quartered

LAKSA PASTE

1 medium brown onion (150g),
    chopped coarsely
⅓ cup (80ml) coconut milk
2 tablespoons lime juice
1 tablespoon shrimp paste
2cm (¾ inch) piece fresh ginger (10g), grated
1 tablespoon macadamias (10g), halved
10cm (4-inch) stick fresh lemon grass (20g),
    chopped finely
4 cloves garlic, quartered
2 fresh small red thai (serrano) chillies,
    chopped coarsely
2 teaspoons each ground coriander and
    ground cumin
1 teaspoon ground turmeric

1 Make laksa paste.
2 Heat oil in a large saucepan over medium heat; cook laksa paste, stirring, for 5 minutes or until fragrant. Add coconut milk, stock, sugar, sauce and lime leaves; bring to the boil. Reduce heat; simmer, covered, for 30 minutes.
3 Meanwhile, shell and devein prawns, leaving tails intact.
4 Place egg noodles in a medium heatproof bowl, cover with boiling water; separate with a fork, drain. Place rice noodles in same bowl, cover with boiling water; stand until tender, drain.
5 Add prawns to laksa; cook, uncovered, until changed in colour. Season to taste.
6 Divide noodles among serving bowls; ladle hot laksa into bowls. Top with sprouts and coriander; serve with lime.

LAKSA PASTE Blend or process ingredients until mixture forms a smooth paste.

nutritional count per serving 55.2g total fat (41.6g saturated fat); 3775kJ (903 cal); 56.6g carbohydrate; 42g protein; 7.6g fibre

notes Recipe is not suitable to freeze.
Shrimp paste, also known as trasi and blanchan, is a strong-scented pungent flavouring.

CHILLED AVOCADO SOUP WITH CRAB

prep + cook time 20 minutes (+ refrigeration) serves 6 as a starter

3 fresh jalapeños or long green chillies
3 green onions (scallions), cut into
   white and green parts
2 cloves garlic
125g (4 ounces) yellow grape tomatoes
2 tablespoons extra virgin olive oil
¼ cup fresh coriander (cilantro), torn
120g (4 ounces) cooked fresh crab meat
⅓ cup (80ml) lime juice
1 cup (250ml) water
2 medium avocados (500g), chopped
¾ cup (210g) greek-style yoghurt

1 Preheat oven to 200°C/400°F.
2 Cut two of the chillies in half lengthways. Roughly chop the white part of the onion; place in a roasting pan with chilli, garlic, tomatoes and half the oil, season with salt; toss to coat. Roast for 15 minutes or until chillies are soft. Cool.
3 Meanwhile, remove seeds from remaining chilli; chop finely. Thinly slice the green part of the onion. Combine chopped chilli, sliced green onion, coriander, crab meat and the remaining oil in a medium bowl. Cover; refrigerate until ready to serve.
4 Blend roasted vegetables with juice, the water, avocado and yoghurt until smooth. Season to taste. Refrigerate until chilled.
5 Ladle chilled soup into bowls; top with crab mixture. Season with freshly ground black pepper.

nutritional count per serving 20.8g total fat (5g saturated fat); 1027kJ (245 cal); 6.3g carbohydrate; 6.4g protein; 2.8g fibre

notes Recipe is not suitable to freeze.
To reduce the intensity of the chillies, remove their seeds and membranes before roasting.

JERUSALEM ARTICHOKE & SMOKED TROUT SOUP

prep + cook time 1¾ hours **serves** 6

¼ cup (60ml) olive oil

1kg (2 pounds) small fresh jerusalem artichokes (approximately 32), trimmed, peeled

20g (¾ ounce) butter

3 shallots (75g), chopped coarsely

1 clove garlic, quartered

2 litres (8 cups) chicken stock

2 tablespoons lemon juice

½ cup (120g) crème fraîche

1 medium smoked trout (375g), flaked, discard any tiny bone fragments

1 tablespoon finely grated lemon rind

1 Preheat oven to 220°C/425°F.

2 Combine oil and artichokes in a large baking dish; season. Roast in oven, turning occasionally, for 1 hour or until artichokes are tender.

3 Melt butter in a large saucepan over medium heat; cook shallot and garlic, stirring, until soft. Add artichokes, stock and juice; bring to the boil. Reduce heat; simmer, uncovered, 10 minutes. Cool 10 minutes.

4 Blend or process soup, in batches, until smooth. [The soup can be made ahead to this stage. Cover; refrigerate overnight.]

5 Return soup to pan; stir over heat until hot. Stir in crème fraîche and trout. Season to taste. Divide soup among serving bowls; sprinkle with rind.

nutritional count per serving 24.2g total fat (9.1g saturated fat); 1637kJ (391 cal); 20g carbohydrate; 21.1g protein; 5.1g fibre

notes Recipe is not suitable to freeze. Jerusalem artichokes, also known as sunchokes, are available in autumn and winter.

SEAFOOD SOUP WITH GREMOLATA

prep + cook time 2 hours **serves** 6

2kg (4 pounds) fish bones

1 medium brown onion (150g), chopped coarsely

1 medium carrot (120g), chopped coarsely

2 stalks celery (300g), trimmed, chopped coarsely

4 litres (16 cups) water

8 black peppercorns

2 dried bay leaves

1 tablespoon olive oil

1 medium brown onion (150g), chopped coarsely, extra

2 cloves garlic, crushed

5 medium tomatoes (750g), chopped coarsely

3 teaspoons white (granulated) sugar

400g (12½ ounces) canned crushed tomatoes

¼ cup (70g) tomato paste

½ cup (125ml) dry white wine

2 medium uncooked lobster tails (330g), shelled, chopped coarsely

400g (12½ ounces) boneless firm white fish fillets, chopped coarsely

GREMOLATA

1 clove garlic, chopped finely

1 tablespoon thinly sliced lemon rind

2 tablespoons thinly sliced fresh flat-leaf parsley leaves

1 Combine fish bones, onion, carrot, celery, the water, peppercorns and bay leaves in a large saucepan. Simmer, uncovered, for 20 minutes. Strain stock over a large bowl; discard bones and vegetables. [Stock can be made ahead to this stage. Cover; refrigerate overnight or freeze.]

2 Heat oil in same cleaned pan over medium heat; cook extra onion and garlic, stirring, until onion softens. Add chopped tomato and sugar; cook, stirring, about 10 minutes or until tomato is soft. Stir in canned tomatoes, paste and wine; bring to the boil. Reduce heat; simmer, uncovered, about 5 minutes or until mixture thickens slightly, stirring occasionally. Add stock; bring to the boil. Reduce heat; simmer, uncovered, for 20 minutes. Cool 10 minutes.

3 Blend or process tomato mixture, in batches, until smooth. Return to same cleaned pan; bring to the boil. Add lobster and fish; simmer, stirring, about 5 minutes or until seafood is just cooked. Season to taste.

4 Make gremolata. Serve soup sprinkled with gremolata.

GREMOLATA Combine ingredients in a small bowl.

---

nutritional count per serving 7.9g total fat (1.7g saturated fat); 1143kJ (273 cal); 15.7g carbohydrate; 30.9g protein; 3.9g fibre

notes Recipe is not suitable to freeze. If you have a citrus zester, use this for the thin slices of lemon rind; it may also be finely grated.

FENNEL, POTATO & SCALLOP SOUP

prep + cook time 1½ hours **serves** 6

5 medium fennel bulbs (1.5kg)
2 tablespoons olive oil
1 medium leek (350g), chopped coarsely
2 stalks celery (300g), trimmed,
  chopped coarsely
1 medium swede (230g), grated coarsely
2 cloves garlic, crushed
1 large potato (300g)
3 cups (750ml) chicken stock
2½ cups (625ml) water
1 cup (250ml) pouring cream
12 scallops, roe removed (300g)
40g (1½ ounces) butter
1 tablespoon lemon juice

CARAMELISED FENNEL

30g (1 ounce) butter
1 small fennel bulb (200g), sliced thinly
1 tablespoon brown sugar
1 tablespoon sherry (optional)

1 Trim fennel, reserving fronds. Coarsely chop fennel.

2 Heat oil in a large saucepan over medium heat; cook fennel, stirring, until soft. Add leek, celery and swede; cook, stirring occasionally, about 15 minutes or until vegetables begin to caramelise. Stir in garlic; cook until fragrant.

3 Coarsely grate potato, add to pan with stock and the water; bring to the boil. Reduce heat; simmer, covered, about 20 minutes or until vegetables are tender. Cool 10 minutes.

4 Meanwhile, make caramelised fennel.

5 Blend or process soup, in batches, until smooth. Season to taste. Strain soup into pan, add half the cream; heat soup over medium heat, stirring occasionally, until hot.

6 Trim scallops; season. Melt butter in a large frying pan; cook scallops, in batches, basting with butter, until edges begin to turn golden. Add juice to pan, spoon mixture over scallops.

7 Ladle soup into serving bowls; top with caramelised fennel and scallops. Drizzle with remaining cream, and sprinkle with reserved fennel fronds.

CARAMELISED FENNEL Melt butter in a medium frying pan; cook fennel, stirring, about 10 minutes or until tender. Stir in sugar; cook, stirring, 5 minutes or until caramelised. Add sherry; cook 1 minute or until mixture thickens. Cover to keep warm.

nutritional count per serving 31.8g total fat (17g saturated fat); 1796kJ (429 cal); 18.4g carbohydrate; 14.6g protein; 6g fibre

notes Recipe not suitable to freeze. Before using, wash leeks under running water to remove any grit from the inside layers.

OYSTER & SAFFRON SOUP

prep + cook time 1 hour **serves** 6

80g (2½ ounces) butter
1 large brown onion (200g),
    chopped coarsely
1 medium leek (350g), chopped coarsely
4 medium potatoes (800g),
    chopped coarsely
6 saffron threads
1.5 litres (6 cups) fish stock
1 litre (4 cups) water
24 oysters (600g), shelled
½ cup (125ml) pouring cream
2 tablespoons lemon juice
¼ cup finely chopped fresh chives

1 Melt butter in a large saucepan over medium heat; cook onion and leek, stirring, about 10 minutes or until soft. Add potato and saffron; cook, stirring, 2 minutes.

2 Add stock and the water; bring to the boil. Reduce heat; simmer, uncovered, for 15 minutes or until potato is tender. Remove from heat, add half the oysters; cool 10 minutes.

3 Blend or process soup mixture, in batches, until smooth. [Soup can be made ahead to this stage. Cover; refrigerate overnight.]

4 Return soup to pan with remaining oysters, cream and juice; stir over heat until hot. Season to taste; stir in chives.

nutritional count per serving 20.7g total fat (12.5g saturated fat); 1419kJ (339 cal); 22.4g carbohydrate; 13.9g protein; 4.1g fibre

notes Recipe is not suitable to freeze. You can substitute ½ teaspoon ground turmeric for the saffron to achieve the right colour.

GRUYERE TOASTS

prep + cook time 10 minutes **makes** 4 slices

Preheat grill (broiler). Cut four thick slices from a small french bread stick (150g). Toast slices on one side under grill. Turn slices over and sprinkle tops with ½ cup finely grated gruyère cheese; place under the grill until the cheese melts.

ANCHOVY TOASTS

prep + cook time 10 minutes **makes** 4 slices

Preheat grill (broiler). Combine 50g (1½oz) softened butter, 6 finely chopped anchovy fillets and 3 tablespoons finely chopped fresh garlic chives in a small bowl. Cut four thick slices from a small french bread stick (150g). Toast slices on one side under grill. Spread untoasted side with anchovy butter; grill until browned lightly.

LEMON FETTA TOASTS

prep + cook time 10 minutes **makes** 4 slices

Preheat grill (broiler). Combine 150g (4½oz) fetta cheese with 1 teaspoon of finely grated lemon rind in a small bowl. Cut four thick slices from a small french bread stick (150g). Place slices on an oven tray. Toast slices one side; turn, sprinkle each slice with fetta mixture and another 1 teaspoon finely grated lemon rind. Grill toasts until browned lightly.

BACON TOASTS

prep + cook time 15 minutes **makes** 4 slices

Preheat grill (broiler). Coarsely chop 2 rindless bacon slices; cook in a heated small frying pan until browned and crisp. Drain on absorbent paper. Cut four thin slices of ciabatta; toast slices on one side under grill. Turn slices and spread with 2 tablespoons wholegrain mustard. Top with bacon and ¼ cup finely grated parmesan; grill until browned lightly.

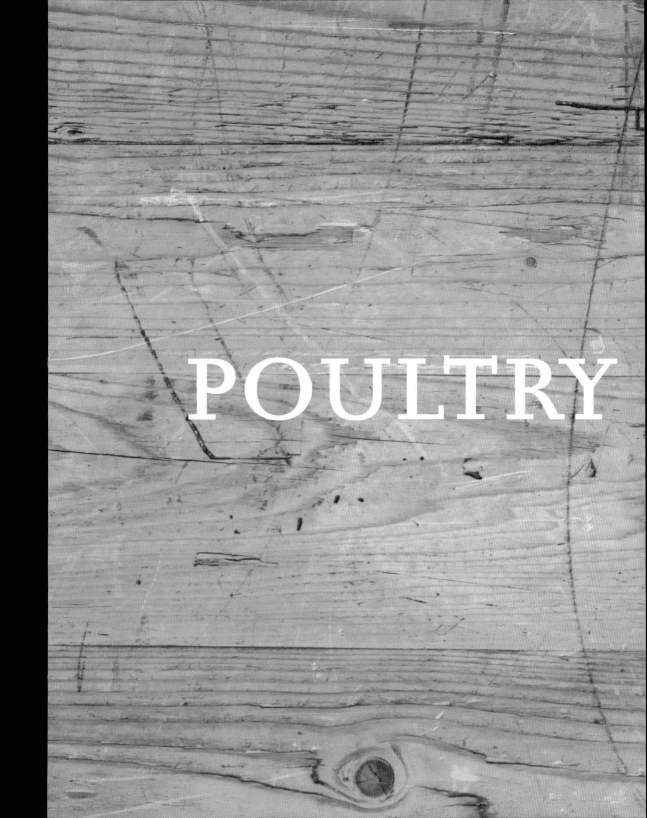

POULTRY

CREAM OF CHICKEN SOUP

prep + cook time 3 hours serves 4

1.8kg (3½-pound) whole chicken
1 medium brown onion (150g),
   chopped coarsely
1 medium carrot (120g), chopped coarsely
1 stalk celery (150g), trimmed,
   chopped coarsely
2 litres (8 cups) water
1 litre (4 cups) chicken stock
40g (1½ ounces) butter
⅓ cup (50g) plain (all-purpose) flour
2 tablespoons lemon juice
½ cup (125ml) pouring cream
¼ cup finely chopped fresh flat-leaf parsley

PARMESAN CHEESE CROÛTONS
1 small french bread stick (150g), cut into
   2cm (¾-inch) slices
½ cup (40g) coarsely grated parmesan

1 Place chicken, onion, carrot and celery in a large saucepan with the water and stock; bring to the boil. Reduce heat; simmer, covered, 1½ hours. Remove chicken from pan; simmer broth, covered, 30 minutes.
2 Strain broth through a muslin-lined sieve or colander into a large heatproof bowl; discard solids.
3 Melt butter in a large saucepan, add flour; cook, stirring, until mixture bubbles and thickens. Gradually stir in broth and juice; bring to the boil. Reduce heat; simmer, uncovered, for 25 minutes or until soup thickens slightly. Remove from heat.
4 Discard skin and bones from chicken; shred meat coarsely. Add chicken and cream to soup; stir over heat, without boiling, until soup is heated through. Season to taste.
5 Meanwhile, make parmesan cheese croûtons. Serve soup with croûtons; sprinkle with parsley.

PARMESAN CHEESE CROÛTONS Preheat grill (broiler). Toast bread on one side; turn over and sprinkle with parmesan. Grill croûtons until cheese browns lightly.

nutritional count per serving 63.8g total fat (28.4g saturated fat); 3984kJ (952 cal); 35.9g carbohydrate; 57.9g protein; 3.8g fibre

notes Recipe is not suitable to freeze. Soup can be made a day ahead; store, covered, in the fridge; make croûtons on day of serving.

SLOW COOKER HOT & SOUR CHICKEN SOUP

prep + cook time 9 hours **serves** 6

1.6kg (3¼-pound) whole chicken
2 medium carrots (240g), chopped coarsely
2 stalks celery (300g), trimmed,
   chopped coarsely
1 large brown onion (200g), chopped coarsely
2.5 litres (10 cups) water
6 fresh kaffir lime leaves, crushed
2 x 10cm (4-inch) stalks lemon grass, bruised
6cm (2½-inch) piece fresh ginger (30g),
   grated coarsely
2 fresh long red chillies, sliced thinly
½ cup (125ml) lime juice
½ cup (125ml) fish sauce
3 teaspoons brown sugar
425g (13½ ounces) canned straw
   mushrooms, rinsed, drained
2 baby buk choy (300g), trimmed,
   chopped coarsely
200g (6½ ounces) rice vermicelli noodles
½ cup firmly packed fresh coriander leaves
   (cilantro)

1 Remove and discard fat and skin from the chicken. Place chicken, carrot, celery, onion and the water in a 4.5-litre (18-cup) slow cooker. Cook, covered, on low, for 8 hours.
2 Carefully remove chicken from cooker; shred the meat coarsely using two forks. Discard bones. Strain cooking liquid through a muslin-lined sieve, clean chux or linen tea towel; discard solids.
3 Return strained liquid to cooker with lime leaves, lemon grass, ginger, chilli, juice, sauce, sugar, mushrooms and chicken. Cook, covered, on high for 30 minutes. Stir in buk choy.
4 Meanwhile, place noodles in a medium heatproof bowl, cover with boiling water; stand 10 minutes or until softened, drain. Divide noodles among serving bowls. Ladle hot soup over noodles. Serve sprinkled with coriander, and fresh sliced chilli, if you like.

nutritional count per serving 16.5g total fat (5g saturated fat); 1482kJ (354 cal); 13.4g carbohydrate; 34.5g protein; 6.2g fibre

notes Recipe is not suitable to freeze. Dense, thumb-sized, straw mushrooms are available canned from Asian grocery stores.

CREAMY CHICKEN CHOWDER

prep + cook time 55 minutes **serves** 4

2 cups (500ml) chicken stock
2 cups (500ml) water
2 chicken breast fillets (400g)
40g (1½ ounces) butter
2 rindless bacon slices (130g),
   chopped coarsely
1 medium brown onion (150g),
   chopped finely
1 clove garlic, crushed
1 medium leek (350g), sliced thinly
1 stalk celery (150g), trimmed,
   chopped finely
¼ cup (35g) plain (all-purpose) flour
2 medium potatoes (400g), chopped coarsely
1 litre (4 cups) milk
½ cup (125ml) pouring cream
2 tablespoons finely chopped fresh chives

1 Bring stock and the water to the boil in a medium saucepan; add chicken, return to the boil. Reduce heat; simmer, covered, about 10 minutes or until chicken is cooked through. Cool chicken in poaching liquid 10 minutes. Remove chicken from pan; discard poaching liquid. Shred chicken coarsely.

2 Melt butter in a large saucepan over medium heat; cook bacon, onion, garlic, leek and celery, stirring, until vegetables soften. Add flour; cook, stirring, until mixture thickens and bubbles. Stir in potato, milk and cream; simmer, covered, about 15 minutes or until potato is tender.

3 Add chicken and chives to soup; cook, stirring, until hot. Season to taste.

nutritional count per serving 37.3g total fat (22.6g saturated fat); 2721kJ (651 cal); 36.1g carbohydrate; 41.7g protein; 4.6g fibre

note Recipe is not suitable to freeze. Before using, leeks should to be washed to remove any grit from the inside layers.

CHICKEN WONTON SOUP

prep + cook time 3 hours (+ refrigeration) **serves** 4

1 tablespoon olive oil

1 medium brown onion (150g),
  chopped coarsely

1 clove garlic, sliced thinly

2cm (¾-inch) piece fresh ginger (10g),
  sliced thinly

1.5 litres (6 cups) water

2 cups (500ml) chicken stock

1kg (2 pounds) chicken bones

1 medium carrot (120g), chopped coarsely

1 stalk celery (150g), chopped coarsely

1 tablespoon light soy sauce

4 green onions (scallions), sliced thinly

CHICKEN WONTONS

150g (4½ ounces) minced (ground) chicken

1 fresh small red thai (serrano) chilli,
  chopped finely

1 clove garlic, crushed

1cm (½-inch) piece fresh ginger (5g), grated

2 teaspoons light soy sauce

1 green onion (scallion), sliced thinly

16 wonton or gow gee wrappers

1 Heat oil in a large saucepan over medium heat; cook brown onion, garlic and ginger, stirring, until onion softens. Add the water, stock, bones, carrot and celery; bring to the boil. Reduce heat; simmer, covered, 2 hours.

2 Strain broth through a muslin-lined sieve or colander into a large heatproof bowl; discard solids. Cool; cover, refrigerate overnight.

3 Make chicken wontons.

4 Skim and discard fat from surface of broth. Return broth to a large saucepan with sauce; bring to the boil. Season to taste. Add wontons, reduce heat; cook about 5 minutes.

5 Divide wontons among bowls; ladle broth into bowls and sprinkle with green onion.

CHICKEN WONTONS Combine chicken, chilli, garlic, ginger, sauce and onion in a small bowl. Place a rounded teaspoon of chicken mixture in centre of each wonton wrapper; brush around edges with a little water, gather edges around filling, pinch together to seal.

nutritional count per serving 5.5g total fat (2g saturated fat); 560kJ (134 cal); 4.7g carbohydrate; 16.6g protein; 0.2g fibre

notes Broth and wontons are suitable to freeze, separately. Double the wonton recipe and pop one batch, sealed tightly, in the freezer.

COMBINATION LONG SOUP

prep + cook time 40 minutes **serves** 4

1 litre (4 cups) water
500g (1 pound) chicken breast fillets
2 litres (8 cups) chicken stock
1 tablespoon japanese soy sauce
2cm (¾-inch) piece fresh ginger (10g), grated
225g (7 ounces) fresh thin wheat noodles
200g (6½ ounces) cooked small prawns
  (shrimp), shelled and deveined
200g (6½ ounces) chinese barbecued pork,
  sliced thinly
4 green onions (scallions), sliced thinly
1 small red capsicum (bell pepper) (150g),
  sliced thinly
100g (3 ounces) mushrooms, sliced thinly
1¼ cups (100g) bean sprouts

1 Bring the water to the boil in a large saucepan; add chicken, return to the boil. Reduce heat; simmer, covered, for 10 minutes or until chicken is cooked. Cool chicken in poaching liquid 10 minutes. Remove chicken from pan; discard poaching liquid. When cool enough to handle, slice chicken thinly.
2 Bring stock, sauce and ginger to the boil in same cleaned pan; add noodles, separating with a fork. Add chicken and remaining ingredients; reduce heat, simmer, uncovered, about 5 minutes or until soup is hot. Season to taste.

nutritional count per serving 26.6g total fat (11.2g saturated fat); 2633kJ (630 cal); 37.9g carbohydrate; 56g protein; 7.8g fibre

notes Recipe is not suitable to freeze. Chinese barbecued pork has a sweet, sticky coating. It is available from Asian grocery stores.

DUCK & LENTIL SOUP

prep + cook time 3¾ hours **serves** 6

1.8kg (3½-pound) whole duck

1.5 litres (6 cups) water

1 litre (4 cups) chicken stock

2 teaspoons olive oil

6 slices pancetta (90g), chopped finely

2 medium carrots (240g), cut into 1cm (½-inch) pieces

2 stalks celery (300g), trimmed, cut into 1cm (½-inch) pieces

1 medium leek (350g), sliced thinly

2 teaspoons black mustard seeds

¾ cup (150g) french-style green lentils

1 Preheat oven to 200°C/400°F.

2 Wash duck under cold water; pat dry inside and out with absorbent paper.

3 Tuck wings under duck. Place duck, breast-side up, on a wire rack in a large baking dish. Prick duck skin with fork several times. Roast, uncovered, about 1½ hours or until cooked through. When cool enough to handle, remove and discard skin from duck; shred meat. Chop bones into large pieces.

4 Combine bones in a large saucepan with the water and stock; bring to the boil. Reduce heat; simmer, uncovered, 35 minutes (skim fat from surface occasionally). Strain broth through a muslin-lined sieve or colander into a large heatproof bowl; discard solids.

5 Heat oil in same cleaned pan over medium heat; cook pancetta, carrot, celery and leek, stirring, about 5 minutes or until vegetables soften. Add seeds and lentils; cook, stirring, 2 minutes. Add broth and duck meat; bring to the boil. Reduce heat; simmer, uncovered, about 25 minutes or until lentils are tender. Season to taste.

nutritional count per serving 60.3g total fat (18.1g saturated fat); 3060kJ (732 cal); 14.6g carbohydrate; 31.5g protein; 6.2g fibre

note Recipe is suitable to freeze. French-style green lentils are great as they retain their firmness after being cooked.

TOM KHA GAI

prep + cook time 45 minutes serves 4

Tom kha gai is a chicken coconut dish from Thailand.

250g (8 ounces) chicken tenderloins
1½ cups (375ml) water
1½ cups (375ml) chicken stock
410ml (13 ounces) canned coconut milk
2cm (¾-inch) piece fresh ginger (10g), peeled, sliced thinly
10cm (4-inch) stick fresh lemon grass (20g), bruised
4 fresh kaffir lime leaves, torn
1 fresh small red thai (serrano) chilli, halved lengthways
¼ cup finely chopped fresh coriander (cilantro) root
2 teaspoons fish sauce
1 teaspoon grated palm sugar
1 tablespoon lime juice
45g (1½ ounces) straw mushrooms, sliced thinly
3 fresh kaffir lime leaves, extra, shredded finely
2 fresh small red thai (serrano) chillies, extra, chopped finely

1 Half-fill a medium frying pan with water, add chicken; bring to the boil. Reduce heat; simmer, covered, about 5 minutes or until chicken is tender. Drain chicken, discard liquid. Chop chicken finely.
2 Meanwhile, place the water, stock, half the coconut milk, and the ginger, lemon grass, lime leaves, chilli, coriander and sauce in a medium saucepan; bring to the boil. Reduce heat; simmer 15 minutes.
3 Strain liquid; discard solids. Return liquid to same pan with remaining coconut milk, sugar, juice, chicken and mushrooms. Reheat until hot, without boiling.
4 Serve soup sprinkled with extra lime leaves and chillies.

nutritional count per serving 24.9g total fat (19.5g saturated fat); 1329kJ (318 cal); 5.7g carbohydrate; 17.4g protein; 2.4g fibre

notes Recipe is not suitable to freeze. If you want to reduce the intensity of the chillies, remove the seeds and membranes.

78

CHICKEN & CORN SOUP

prep + cook time 40 minutes **serves** 4

cooking-oil spray
2 trimmed corn cobs (500g), kernels
   removed
4cm (1½-inch) piece fresh ginger (20g),
   grated coarsely
2 cloves garlic, crushed
4 green onions (scallions), sliced thinly
1 litre (4 cups) water
1 litre (4 cups) chicken stock
200g (6½ ounces) chicken breast fillet
1 teaspoon light soy sauce
1 egg white, beaten lightly

1 Lightly spray a heated large saucepan with cooking oil; cook corn, ginger, garlic and half the onion, stirring, until fragrant. Add the water and stock; bring to the boil.
2 Add chicken, reduce heat; simmer, covered, about 10 minutes or until chicken is cooked. Cool chicken in broth 10 minutes. Remove chicken; shred meat finely.
3 Return broth to the boil; add chicken and soy sauce. Reduce heat, and gradually stir in egg white.
4 Serve soup sprinkled with remaining onion.

nutritional count per serving 3.2g total fat (0.9g saturated fat); 769kJ (184 cal); 17.4g carbohydrate; 18.9g protein; 4.6g fibre

notes Recipe is not suitable to freeze. You can use 2 cups of frozen corn kernels rather than trimming fresh corn cobs, if you prefer.

CHICKEN & RISONI SOUP WITH HERBED MEATBALLS

prep + cook time 3¼ hours (+ refrigeration) **serves** 4

You need to start this recipe the day before serving.

2.5 litres (10 cups) water
1.6kg (3¼-pound) whole chicken
1 large tomato (220g), halved
2 stalks celery (300g), trimmed, halved
1 medium brown onion (150g), halved
2 stalks fresh flat-leaf parsley
5 black peppercorns
300g (9½ ounces) minced (ground) chicken
½ cup (50g) packaged breadcrumbs
2 tablespoons finely chopped fresh
   flat-leaf parsley
2 tablespoons finely grated parmesan
1 egg
1 tablespoon olive oil
¾ cup (165g) risoni pasta
2 tablespoons lemon juice
⅓ cup coarsely chopped fresh
   flat-leaf parsley

1 Place the water, whole chicken, tomato, celery, onion, parsley stalks and peppercorns in a large saucepan; bring to the boil. Reduce heat; simmer, covered, 2 hours.
2 Remove chicken from pan. Strain broth through a muslin-lined sieve or colander into a large heatproof bowl; discard solids. Allow broth to cool, cover; refrigerate overnight. When chicken is cool enough to handle, remove and discard skin and bones. Shred meat coarsely; cover, refrigerate overnight.
3 Combine minced chicken, breadcrumbs, finely chopped parsley, cheese and egg in a medium bowl; roll rounded teaspoons of mixture into balls. Heat oil in a medium saucepan; cook meatballs, in batches, until browned all over.
4 Skim and discard fat from surface of broth. Place broth in a large saucepan; bring to the boil. Reduce heat; simmer, uncovered, 20 minutes. Add meatballs and pasta; simmer, uncovered, about 10 minutes or until meatballs are cooked through and pasta is tender. Add 2 cups of the reserved chicken meat (keep remaining chicken for another use), juice and coarsely chopped parsley to pan; stir soup over medium heat until hot. Season to taste.

nutritional count per serving 45.8g total fat (3.7g saturated fat); 3536kJ (846 cal); 40.4g carbohydrate; 66.3g protein; 4.3g fibre

notes Broth and meatballs suitable to freeze, separately. Also known as risi, risoni is a very small, rice-shaped pasta similar to orzo.

PRESSURE COOKER CHICKEN & RICE SOUP

prep + cook time 30 minutes **serves** 4

2 teaspoons olive oil

1 large brown onion (200g), chopped finely

⅓ cup (65g) white long-grain rice

1 large tomato (220g), chopped finely

1 tablespoon drained, finely chopped, pickled jalapeño chillies

1 cup coarsely chopped fresh coriander (cilantro)

1 large avocado (320g), chopped finely

CHICKEN STOCK

½ whole uncooked chicken (800g)

1 medium carrot (120g), halved

1 small brown onion (80g), halved

1 stalk celery (150g), halved

1 teaspoon black peppercorns

1.5 litres (6 cups) water

1 Make chicken stock. Discard skin and bones from chicken; shred meat coarsely.

2 Heat oil in a 6-litre (24-cup) pressure cooker; cook onion, stirring, until soft. Add rice; stir to coat in onion mixture. Add stock; secure lid. Bring cooker to high pressure according to manufacturer's instructions. Reduce heat to stabilise pressure; cook for 5 minutes.

3 Release the steam pressure according manufacturer's instructions; remove lid. Return chicken to cooker with tomato and chilli; simmer, uncovered, until hot. Stir in coriander; season to taste. Serve soup topped with avocado.

CHICKEN STOCK Combine ingredients in a 6-litre (24-cup) pressure cooker; secure lid. Bring cooker to high pressure according to manufacturer's instructions. Reduce heat to stabilise pressure; cook 15 minutes. Release the steam pressure according to manufacturer's instructions; remove lid. Strain stock into a large heatproof bowl. Reserve chicken; discard solids.

nutritional count per serving 13.4g total fat (3g saturated fat); 950kJ (227 cal); 18.4g carbohydrate; 4g protein; 4.2g fibre

notes Recipe is not suitable to freeze. Always check the manufacturer's instructions before using a pressure cooker.

CHICKEN, CORN & NOODLE SOUP

prep + cook time 30 minutes **serves** 4

1 tablespoon vegetable oil

1 medium brown onion (150g), chopped finely

2 cloves garlic, crushed

3cm (1¼-inch) piece fresh ginger (15g), grated coarsely

1 litre (4 cups) chicken stock

2 cups (500ml) water

125g (4 ounces) canned creamed corn

420g (13½ ounces) canned corn kernels, rinsed, drained

125g (4 ounces) dried wheat noodles

350g (11 ounces) chicken breast fillets, sliced thinly

2 tablespoons japanese soy sauce

100g (3 ounces) baby spinach leaves

4 green onions (scallions), chopped coarsely

1 Heat oil in a large saucepan over medium heat; cook brown onion, garlic and ginger, stirring, for 5 minutes or until onion softens.

2 Add stock, the water, creamed corn and corn kernels to the pan, cover; bring to the boil over high heat.

3 Reduce heat to medium-low; simmer, uncovered, for 5 minutes.

4 Carefully break the noodles in half and add to the pan. Simmer, uncovered, for 2 minutes. Stir to separate noodles.

5 Add chicken to the pan with soy sauce; simmer, uncovered, 1 minute or until chicken is cooked through. Add extra soy sauce to taste, if needed.

6 Stir in spinach; season to taste. Using a ladle, divide the soup between bowls. Sprinkle with green onion.

nutritional count per serving 7.8g total fat (1.5g saturated fat); 1664kJ (398 cal); 47.9g carbohydrate; 30.7g protein; 6.3g fibre

notes Recipe is not suitable to freeze. Japanese soy sauce is an all-purpose low-sodium sauce; it is the one often used as a condiment.

CHICKEN LAKSA

prep + cook time 25 minutes **serves** 4

1 tablespoon vegetable oil
400g (12½ ounces) chicken thigh fillets,
   sliced thinly
⅓ cup (100g) laksa paste
1½ cups (375ml) chicken stock
½ cup (125ml) water
270ml can coconut milk
200g (6½ ounces) bean thread noodles
½ cup loosely packed fresh coriander leaves
   (cilantro)

1 Heat oil in a large saucepan over medium heat; cook chicken, in two batches, turning for 3 minutes, or until browned lightly. Remove from pan.

2 Cook paste in same pan, stirring, about 3 minutes or until fragrant. Return chicken to pan with stock, the water and coconut milk; bring to the boil. Reduce heat; simmer, uncovered, 10 minutes or until chicken is cooked. Season to taste.

3 Meanwhile, place noodles in a medium heatproof bowl, cover with boiling water; stand until noodles are tender, separate with a fork. Drain.

4 Divide noodles between bowls; ladle hot laksa over top of noodles. Serve sprinkled with coriander.

nutritional count per serving 29.6g total fat (15.4g saturated fat); 1789kJ (428 cal); 15.8g carbohydrate; 23.4g protein; 4.3g fibre

notes Recipe is not suitable to freeze. Some laksa pastes are very hot, so if you have a low heat tolerance, use less than stated here.

SLOW COOKER CHICKEN MULLIGATAWNY

prep + cook time 8½ hours **serves** 4

2 medium brown onions (300g), chopped coarsely
2 cloves garlic, chopped coarsely
2 medium carrots (240g), chopped coarsely
1 stalk celery (150g), trimmed, chopped coarsely
1 fresh long red chilli, chopped coarsely
4cm (1½-inch) piece fresh ginger (20g), grated coarsely
2 chicken marylands (700g)
1 tablespoon mild curry powder
1 teaspoon each ground cumin and garam masala
3 cups (750ml) chicken stock
1 cup (250ml) coconut milk
½ cup loosely packed fresh coriander leaves (cilantro)

1 Place onion, garlic, carrot, celery, chilli, ginger, chicken, curry powder, cumin, garam masala and stock in a 4.5-litre (18-cup) slow cooker. Cook, covered, on low, for 8 hours.
2 Carefully remove chicken from the cooker; discard the skin and bones. Shred meat coarsely using two forks.
3 Skim fat from the surface of the vegetable mixture. Blend or process vegetable mixture until smooth. Return chicken to the pan with the coconut milk; stir to combine.
4 Serve soup sprinkled with coriander, and drizzle with extra coconut milk, if you like.

nutritional count per serving 20.4g total fat (13.4g saturated fat); 1437kJ (343 cal); 11.1g carbohydrate; 27g protein; 5.3g fibre

notes Recipe is not suitable to freeze. Chicken marylands have the leg and thigh still connected in a single piece.

CHICKEN TIPS

CHICKEN SOUP HAS A BIG REPUTATION: IT'S THE GO-TO SOUP FOR A COLD OR FLU, IS THE BEST SOUP TO COMFORT YOU WHEN FEELING DOWN, OR TO WARM YOU UP ON A COLD WINTER'S DAY. WHEN USING A

WHOLE CHICKEN, BLOT UP THE FAT THAT RISES TO THE SURFACE FOR A LOWER-FAT VERSION. REFRIGERATE THE SOUP OVERNIGHT TO SOLIDIFY THE FAT, MAKING IT EASY TO REMOVE.

COCONUT, CHICKEN & KAFFIR LIME SOUP

prep + cook time 1 hour **serves** 4

1 tablespoon peanut oil

600g (1¼ pounds) chicken thigh fillets,
    cut into 1cm (½-inch) strips

¼ cup (75g) green curry paste

1 litre (4 cups) chicken stock

800ml can coconut milk

1 fresh long green chilli, chopped finely

8 fresh kaffir lime leaves, shredded

125g (4 ounces) rice vermicelli

2 tablespoons grated palm sugar

2 tablespoons lime juice

2 tablespoons fish sauce

1 cup (80g) bean sprouts

½ cup loosely packed vietnamese mint leaves

1 fresh long green chilli, extra, sliced thinly

2 limes, cut into thin wedges

1 Heat oil in a large saucepan over medium heat; cook chicken, in batches, 5 minutes or until browned lightly. Remove from pan.

2 Place paste in same pan; cook, stirring, until fragrant. Return chicken to pan with stock, coconut milk, chopped chilli and lime leaves; bring to the boil. Reduce heat; simmer, uncovered, 30 minutes, skimming fat from surface occasionally. Add vermicelli; cook, uncovered, until vermicelli is just tender. Stir in sugar, juice and sauce. Season to taste.

3 Serve soup sprinkled with sprouts, mint, sliced chilli and lime.

nutritional count per serving 63.9g total fat (41.6g saturated fat); 3478kJ (832 cal); 25g carbohydrate; 38g protein; 6.8g fibre

notes Recipe is not suitable to freeze. Vietnamese mint is not a mint, but a narrow-leafed, pungent herb, also known as laksa leaf.

94

CHICKEN, CHORIZO & OKRA GUMBO

prep + cook time 3¼ hours serves 8

1.5kg (3-pound) whole chicken
2 medium carrots (240g), chopped coarsely
2 stalks celery (300g), trimmed,
    chopped coarsely
1 medium brown onion (150g),
    chopped coarsely
12 black peppercorns
1 dried bay leaf
3 litres (12 cups) water
60g (2 ounces) butter
1 small brown onion (80g), extra,
    chopped finely
2 cloves garlic, crushed
1 medium red capsicum (bell pepper)
    (200g), chopped finely
2 teaspoons dried oregano
1 teaspoon sweet paprika
¼ teaspoon each cayenne pepper and
    ground cloves
¼ cup (35g) plain (all-purpose) flour
¼ cup (70g) tomato paste
400g (12½ ounces) canned crushed
    tomatoes
100g (3 ounces) fresh okra, halved diagonally
1 cup (200g) white medium-grain rice
1 cured chorizo sausage (170g), sliced thinly

1 Place chicken in a large saucepan with carrot, celery, onion, peppercorns, bay leaf and the water; bring to the boil. Reduce heat; simmer, covered, for 1½ hours.
2 Remove chicken from pan. Strain broth through a muslin-lined sieve or colander into a large heatproof bowl; discard solids. When chicken is cool enough to handle, remove and discard skin and bones; shred meat coarsely.
3 Melt butter in a large saucepan over medium heat; cook extra onion and garlic, stirring, until onion softens. Add capsicum, oregano and spices; cook, stirring, until fragrant. Add flour and paste; cook, stirring, 1 minute. Gradually stir in broth and tomatoes; bring to the boil, stirring. Stir in okra and rice; simmer, uncovered, stirring occasionally, for 15 minutes or until rice is tender.
4 Heat a large oiled frying pan; cook sausage until browned, drain.
5 Add sausage and chicken to gumbo; stir over medium heat until hot. Season to taste.

nutritional count per serving 26.8g total fat (5.7g saturated fat); 2011kJ (481 cal); 30.5g carbohydrate; 27.8g protein; 3.9g fibre

notes Recipe is not suitable to freeze. Okra is a long, slender, ridged pod with a furry skin; when cut it releases a sticky substance.

CHICKEN, PEA & ASPARAGUS SOUP WITH PISTOU

prep + cook time 30 minutes **serves** 4

You need 450g (14½ ounces) of fresh peas in the pod or 2 cups (240g) frozen peas for this recipe.

3 cups (750ml) chicken stock
3 cups (750ml) water
1 clove garlic, crushed
¼ teaspoon coarsely ground black pepper
400g (12½ ounces) chicken breast fillets
170g (5½ ounces) asparagus, trimmed, chopped coarsely
1½ cups (240g) shelled fresh peas
1 tablespoon lemon juice

PISTOU
½ cup coarsely chopped fresh flat-leaf parsley
½ cup coarsely chopped fresh mint
¼ cup coarsely chopped fresh garlic chives
2 teaspoons finely grated lemon rind
1 clove garlic, crushed
2 teaspoons olive oil

1 Bring stock, the water, garlic and pepper to the boil in a large saucepan. Add chicken; return to the boil. Reduce heat; simmer, covered, about 10 minutes or until chicken is cooked through. Cool in broth 10 minutes. Remove chicken from pan; slice thinly.
2 Meanwhile, make pistou.
3 Add remaining ingredients to broth; bring to the boil. Return chicken to pan; simmer, uncovered, about 3 minutes or until vegetables are just tender. Season to taste.
4 Serve soup topped with pistou.

PISTOU Pound ingredients using a mortar and pestle until smooth.

nutritional count per serving 5.7g total fat (1.3g saturated fat); 861kJ (206 cal); 7.3g carbohydrate; 28.9g protein; 4.4g fibre

notes Recipe is suitable to freeze. Pistou can be frozen but may discolour when defrosted, so it's best made on the day of serving.

TOMATO, CORN & CHILLI CHICKEN SOUP

prep + cook time 30 minutes **serves** 6

2 tablespoons olive oil

2 chicken breast fillets (400g)

1 medium red onion (170g), chopped finely

1 tablespoon plain (all-purpose) flour

1.5 litres (6 cups) chicken stock

2 cups (500ml) tomato juice

420g (13 ounces) canned corn kernels, rinsed, drained

2 fresh small red thai (serrano) chillies, chopped finely

¼ cup loosely packed fresh coriander leaves (cilantro)

1 Heat half the oil in a large saucepan over medium-high heat; cook chicken until cooked through. When cool enough to handle, shred chicken into small pieces.

2 Heat remaining oil in same pan over medium heat; cook onion, stirring, until soft. Add flour; cook, stirring, until mixture bubbles and thickens. Gradually stir in stock and juice; cook, stirring, until mixture boils and thickens slightly.

3 Add chicken, corn and chilli; stir over heat until soup is hot. Season to taste. Just before serving, sprinkle with coriander.

nutritional count per serving 8.6g total fat (1.7g saturated fat); 957kJ (229 cal); 18.3g carbohydrate; 18.3g protein; 2.6g fibre

notes Recipe is suitable to freeze. A skinned, boned and shredded bbq chicken can be substituted for the chicken breasts.

AVGOLEMONO
(GREEK LEMON & RICE SOUP)

prep + cook time 50 minutes **serves** 4

2 teaspoons olive oil

1 small brown onion (80g), chopped finely

1 litre (4 cups) chicken stock

400g (12½ ounces) chicken breast fillets, chopped coarsely

⅓ cup (65g) white short-grain rice

2 eggs

⅓ cup (80ml) lemon juice

2 tablespoons finely chopped fresh flat-leaf parsley

1 Heat oil in a large saucepan over medium heat; cook onion, stirring, until soft. Add stock, chicken and rice; bring to the boil. Reduce heat; simmer, covered, 20 minutes or until rice is tender.

2 Whisk eggs and juice in a small bowl until smooth. Gradually whisk ½ cup hot soup into egg mixture then stir warmed egg mixture into soup. Season to taste.

3 Serve soup sprinkled with parsley.

nutritional count per serving 8.4g total fat (2.3g saturated fat); 1099kJ (263 cal); 16.3g carbohydrate; 30.3g protein; 0.5g fibre

notes Recipe is not suitable to freeze. Arborio rice is an excellent choice to use here as its high starch level makes for a creamy soup.

THAI CHICKEN BROTH WITH CHICKEN WONTONS

prep + cook time 2½ hours (+ refrigeration) **serves** 6

4 litres (16 cups) water

2kg (4 pounds) chicken bones

2 medium brown onions (300g), chopped coarsely

½ cup coarsely chopped fresh lemon grass

4cm (1½-inch) piece fresh ginger (20g), chopped coarsely

2 fresh long red chillies, halved crossways

2 cloves garlic, quartered

1 teaspoon black peppercorns

300g (9½ ounces) minced (ground) chicken

1 clove garlic, crushed

2 teaspoons finely chopped fresh coriander (cilantro)

2cm (¾-inch) piece fresh ginger (10g), grated

1 fresh small red thai (serrano) chilli, seeded, chopped finely

¼ cup (60ml) japanese soy sauce

30 wonton wrappers

1 egg white

1 tablespoon lime juice

1 tablespoon mirin

1 cup firmly packed trimmed watercress sprigs

3 green onions (scallions), sliced thinly

2 fresh long red chillies, seeded, sliced thinly

⅓ cup loosely packed fresh coriander (cilantro) leaves

1 Combine the water, chicken bones, brown onion, lemon grass, chopped ginger, halved chilli, quartered garlic and peppercorns in a large saucepan; bring to the boil. Reduce heat; simmer, uncovered, 2½ hours. Strain broth through a muslin-lined sieve or colander into a large bowl; discard solids. Allow broth to cool, cover; refrigerate until cold.

2 Combine minced chicken, crushed garlic, chopped coriander, grated ginger, chopped chilli and 1 tablespoon of the soy sauce in a medium bowl. Place 1 rounded teaspoon of the chicken mixture in the centre of each wrapper; brush around edges with egg white, gather edges around filling, pinch together to seal. Repeat process with remaining filling and wrappers.

3 Skim fat from surface of broth; place broth in large saucepan; bring to the boil. Cook wontons, in two batches, for 4 minutes or until cooked through. Using slotted spoon, transfer wontons from pan to individual serving bowls. Stir remaining soy sauce, juice and mirin into broth; return to the boil. Season to taste.

4 Top wontons with watercress, green onion, sliced chilli and coriander leaves; ladle broth into bowls.

---

nutritional count per serving 7.4g total fat (2.7g saturated fat); 1195kJ (286 cal); 30.4g carbohydrate; 23.9g protein; 1.7g fibre

notes Broth and uncooked wontons can be frozen, separately, for up to 3 months; wontons can be cooked in the broth from frozen.

DUCK & MUSHROOM SOUP

prep + cook time 40 minutes (+ standing) **serves** 6

20g (¾ ounce) dried shiitake mushrooms
15g (½ ounce) dried black fungus
1kg (2-pound) chinese barbecued duck
1 litre (4 cups) water
1 litre (4 cups) chicken stock
2 teaspoons grated palm sugar
1 tablespoon mushroom soy sauce
230g (7 ounces) canned bamboo shoots,
   rinsed, drained
100g (3 ounce) swiss brown mushrooms,
   sliced thinly
1 tablespoon cornflour (cornstarch)
1 tablespoon water, extra
4 green onions (scallions), sliced thinly

1 Cover dried shiitake mushrooms and dried fungus in a small bowl with cold water; stand 1 hour. Drain; slice thinly.
2 Meanwhile, remove bones from duck; reserve skin, slice meat thinly.
3 Preheat grill (broiler).
4 Combine the water and stock in a large saucepan; bring to the boil. Add duck, all the mushrooms, sugar, sauce and bamboo shoots to pan; return to the boil.
5 Place duck skin, in a single layer, on an oven tray; grill about 5 minutes or until crisp. Discard excess fat; chop skin coarsely.
6 Meanwhile, blend cornflour with the extra water in a small bowl, add to soup; stir until mixture thickens slightly. Season to taste. Serve soup topped with duck skin and onion.

nutritional count per serving 22.4g total fat (6.8g saturated fat); 1246kJ (298 cal); 4.7g carbohydrate; 19.5g protein; 1.1g fibre

notes Recipe is not suitable to freeze. Dried black fungus adds a crunchy texture to dishes; it is available from Asian greengrocers.

CANTONESE CHICKEN DUMPLING SOUP

prep + cook time 1 hour (+ standing) **serves** 4

10 dried shiitake mushrooms
2 teaspoons peanut oil
2 cloves garlic, crushed
2cm (¾-inch) piece fresh ginger (10g), grated
1 litre (4 cups) water
1 litre (4 cups) chicken stock
2 tablespoons dark soy sauce
200g (6½ ounces) baby corn, halved lengthways
150g (4½ ounces) bean sprouts
3 green onions (scallions), sliced thickly on the diagonal

CHICKEN DUMPLINGS
1 tablespoon peanut oil
1 green onion (scallion), sliced thinly
2cm (¾-inch) piece fresh ginger (10g), grated
1 fresh long red chilli, chopped finely
200g (6½ ounces) minced (ground) chicken
1 teaspoon dark soy sauce
20 wonton wrappers

1 Cover mushrooms with ½ cup cold water in a small bowl; stand 15 minutes. Drain over small bowl; reserve soaking liquid. Slice mushrooms thinly.
2 Meanwhile, make chicken dumplings.
3 Heat oil in a large saucepan over medium heat; cook garlic and ginger, stirring, for 2 minutes. Stir in the water, stock, sauce and reserved soaking liquid; bring to the boil. Reduce heat; simmer, uncovered, for 15 minutes.
4 Add mushrooms, dumplings and corn to soup; bring to the boil. Reduce heat; simmer, about 10 minutes or until dumplings are cooked through. Season to taste.
5 Serve bowls of soup sprinkled with sprouts and onion.

CHICKEN DUMPLINGS Heat oil in a medium frying pan over medium heat; cook onion, ginger and chilli, stirring, until onion softens. Add mince; cook, stirring, until browned. Stir in sauce; cool. Place a rounded teaspoon of mixture in the centre of each wrapper; brush edges with a little water. Gather edges around filling, pinch together to seal.

nutritional count per serving 13.3g total fat (3.2g saturated fat); 1354kJ (324 cal); 28.2g carbohydrate; 20g protein; 5.6g fibre

notes Soup and dumplings are suitable to freeze separately. Bring the soup to the boil and cook the dumplings from frozen.

109

CHICKEN & MUSHROOM RAVIOLI IN BROTH

prep + cook time 4 hours **serves** 6

1kg (2 pounds) chicken bones
1 medium brown onion (150g),
   chopped coarsely
1 medium carrot (120g), chopped coarsely
1 stalk celery (150g), trimmed
   chopped coarsely
1 tablespoon olive oil
2.5 litres (10 cups) water
10g (½ ounce) dried porcini mushrooms
8 fresh lasagne sheets (375g)
1 egg, beaten lightly
100g (3 ounces) swiss brown mushrooms,
   sliced thickly
100g (3 ounces) baby spinach
½ cup (40g) shaved parmesan

CHICKEN AND MUSHROOM FILLING

100g (3 ounces) flat mushrooms
80g (2½ ounces) button mushrooms
1 tablespoon olive oil
1 clove garlic, crushed
1 teaspoon lemon thyme leaves
½ cup (80g) finely chopped cooked chicken
2 teaspoons finely grated lemon rind
125g (4 ounces) mascarpone cheese

1 Preheat oven to 220°C/425°F.
2 Place bones, onion, carrot and celery in a large baking dish; drizzle with oil. Roast for 1 hour or until well browned. Transfer to a large stockpot. Add the water and porcini mushrooms; bring to the boil. Reduce heat; simmer, uncovered, 2 hours or until liquid is reduced by half. Strain through a fine sieve into a large heatproof bowl; discard solids.
3 Make chicken and mushroom filling.
4 Dip lasagne sheets briefly into cold water to prevent cracking. Cut 48 x 8cm (3¼-inch) rounds from sheets. Brush half the rounds with egg; top with 2 teaspoons of filling. Place remaining rounds over filling; press to seal.
5 Cook ravioli, in batches, in a large saucepan of simmering salted water for 2 minutes or until ravioli float to the top. Remove with a slotted spoon; cover to keep warm.
6 Meanwhile, bring stock to the boil, add swiss brown mushrooms and spinach; cook for 2 minutes or until mushrooms are tender. Season to taste.
7 Divide ravioli and stock mixture between serving bowls; top with parmesan.

CHICKEN AND MUSHROOM FILLING Process mushrooms until finely chopped. Heat oil in a medium frying pan over high heat, add mushrooms, garlic and thyme; cook, stirring, 5 minutes or until any liquid evaporates. Stir in chicken and rind; cool. Stir in mascarpone; season to taste.

nutritional count per serving 16.5g total fat (8.6g saturated fat); 1216kJ (290 cal); 21.1g carbohydrate; 13.8g protein; 2.5g fibre

notes Stock can be made 3 days ahead; store, covered, in the fridge. Ravioli can be made 3 hours ahead; refrigerate, covered with a damp tea towel.

THAI CHICKEN NOODLE BROTH

prep + cook time 30 minutes **serves** 4

1 litre (4 cups) chicken stock
2 cups (500ml) water
3cm (1¼-inch) piece fresh ginger (15g),
    grated coarsely
1 fresh small red thai (serrano) chilli,
    chopped finely
400g (12½ ounces) chicken breast fillets,
    sliced thinly
400g (12½ ounces) fresh rice noodles
1 tablespoon fish sauce
1 tablespoon grated palm sugar
1 tablespoon lime juice
2 baby buk choy (300g), quartered
⅓ cup loosely packed fresh thai basil leaves

1 Combine stock, the water, ginger and chilli in a large saucepan, cover; bring to the boil. Reduce heat; simmer 5 minutes. Add chicken, noodles, sauce, sugar and juice; simmer, about 5 minutes or until chicken is cooked through and noodles are tender. Season to taste.

2 Divide buk choy among serving bowls; ladle chicken broth into bowls. Sprinkle with basil.

nutritional count per serving 7.1g total fat (2.2g saturated fat); 1208kJ (289 cal); 27.5g carbohydrate; 27.6g protein; 1.7g fibre

notes Recipe is not suitable to freeze.
Thai basil, also known as horapa, has small leaves, purplish stems, and a slight aniseed taste.

SLOW COOKER CHICKEN, PORCINI & BARLEY SOUP

prep + cook time 6½ hours (+ standing) **serves** 4

20g (¾ ounce) dried porcini mushrooms
1 cup (250ml) boiling water
2 chicken marylands (700g)
1 medium brown onion (150g),
    chopped finely
2 cloves garlic, crushed
1 litre (4 cups) chicken stock
½ cup (100g) pearl barley
1 sprig fresh rosemary
1 sprig fresh thyme
1 medium parsnip (250g), chopped finely
1 small kumara (orange sweet potato)
    (250g), chopped finely
2 stalks celery (300g), trimmed,
    chopped finely
250g (8 ounces) swiss brown mushrooms,
    quartered
½ cup finely chopped fresh flat-leaf parsley

1 Place porcini mushrooms in a small heatproof bowl with the water; stand 15 minutes or until softened. Drain, reserve porcini and the soaking liquid.
2 Meanwhile, discard as much skin as possible from the chicken. Place chicken, onion, garlic, stock, barley, rosemary, thyme, parsnip, kumara, celery, swiss brown and porcini mushrooms and reserved soaking liquid into a 4.5-litre (18-cup) slow cooker. Cook, covered, on low, for 6 hours.
3 Remove chicken from cooker. When cool enough to handle, remove meat from bone; shred coarsely. Discard bones. Return meat to cooker; season to taste. Serve topped with parsley.

nutritional count per serving 9.4g total fat (3g saturated fat); 1488kJ (356 cal); 38.9g carbohydrate; 29.2g protein; 8.4g fibre

notes Recipe suitable to freeze for 3 months. Thaw overnight in the fridge before reheating on the stove or in a microwave oven on medium.

MOROCCAN CHICKEN & CHICKPEA SOUP

prep + cook time 1½ hours **serves** 6

2 tablespoons olive oil

340g (11 ounces) chicken breast fillets

1 large brown onion (200g), chopped finely

2 cloves garlic, crushed

2.5cm (1-inch) piece fresh ginger (10g),
   grated coarsely

1½ teaspoons each ground cumin and
   ground coriander

1 teaspoon ground turmeric

½ teaspoon sweet paprika

1 cinnamon stick

¼ cup (35g) plain flour

1 litre (4 cups) chicken stock

1 litre (4 cups) water

600g (1¼ pounds) canned chickpeas
   (garbanzo beans), rinsed, drained

800g (1½ pounds) canned crushed tomatoes

2 tablespoons finely chopped preserved
   lemon rind

¼ cup loosely packed fresh coriander
   leaves (cilantro)

1 Heat half the oil in a large frying pan over medium-high heat; cook chicken for 10 minutes or until browned both sides and cooked through. Drain chicken on absorbent paper, cool 10 minutes; using two forks, shred chicken coarsely.

2 Heat remaining oil in a large saucepan over medium heat; cook onion, garlic and ginger, stirring, until onion softens. Add spices; cook, stirring, until fragrant.

3 Add flour; cook, stirring, until mixture bubbles and thickens. Gradually stir in stock and the water; cook, stirring, until mixture boils and thickens slightly. Reduce heat; simmer, uncovered, 20 minutes.

4 Add chickpeas and tomatoes; bring to the boil. Reduce heat; simmer, uncovered, 10 minutes. [Soup can be made ahead to this stage. Cover; refrigerate overnight.]

5 Add chicken and preserved lemon; stir over heat until soup is hot. Season to taste. Just before serving, stir in fresh coriander.

SERVING SUGGESTION Serve with fattoush (a Middle-Eastern bread salad).

nutritional count per serving 12g total fat (2.3g saturated fat); 1184kJ (283 cal); 20.7g carbohydrate; 19.6g protein; 6.4g fibre

notes Recipe is not suitable to freeze.
To use preserved lemon rind, discard pulp, squeeze juice from rind; rinse rind well, then chop finely.

CHICKEN & VEGETABLE SOUP

prep + cook time 2¾ hours (+ refrigeration) serves 6

You need to start this recipe a day before serving.

1.5kg (3-pound) whole chicken
1 small brown onion (80g), halved
2 litres (8 cups) water
5 black peppercorns
2 dried bay leaves
20g (¾ ounce) butter
2 stalks celery (300g), trimmed, sliced thinly
2 medium carrots (240g), cut into 1cm
    (½-inch) pieces
1 large potato (300g), cut into 1cm
    (½-inch) pieces
150g (4½ ounces) snow peas, trimmed,
    chopped coarsely
3 green onions (scallions), sliced thinly
310g (10 ounces) canned corn kernels,
    rinsed, drained

1 Place chicken, brown onion, the water, peppercorns and bay leaves in a large saucepan; bring to the boil. Reduce heat; simmer, covered, 2 hours.

2 Remove chicken from pan. Strain broth through a muslin-lined sieve or colander into a large bowl; discard solids. Allow broth to cool, cover; refrigerate overnight. When chicken is cool enough to handle, remove and discard skin and bones. Shred meat coarsely; cover, refrigerate overnight.

3 Melt butter in a large saucepan over medium heat; cook celery, carrot and potato, stirring, 2 minutes.

4 Skim and discard fat from surface of the broth. Add to pan; bring to the boil. Reduce heat; simmer, covered, 10 minutes or until vegetables are tender.

5 Add snow peas, green onion, corn and reserved chicken to soup; cook, covered, 5 minutes or until heated through. Season to taste.

nutritional count per serving 9.2g total fat (2.8g saturated fat); 1183kJ (283 cal); 18.8g carbohydrate; 29.1g protein; 4.2g fibre

notes Recipe is not suitable to freeze. Black peppercorns have a slightly hot taste with a hint of sweetness.

SLOW COOKER ITALIAN CHICKEN SOUP

prep + cook time 9 hours **serves** 6

1.5kg (3-pound) whole chicken
3 large tomatoes (650g)
1 medium brown onion (150g),
　chopped coarsely
2 stalks celery (300g), trimmed,
　chopped coarsely
1 large carrot (180g), chopped coarsely
2 dried bay leaves
4 cloves garlic, halved
6 black peppercorns
2 litres (8 cups) water
¾ cup (155g) risoni pasta
½ cup coarsely chopped fresh flat-leaf parsley
½ cup coarsely chopped fresh basil
2 tablespoons finely chopped fresh oregano
¼ cup (60ml) fresh lemon juice

1 Remove then discard as much skin as possible from the chicken. Chop 1 tomato coarsely. Chop remaining tomatoes finely; refrigerate, covered, until required.
2 Place chicken, coarsely chopped tomato, onion, celery, carrot, bay leaves, garlic, peppercorns and the water in a 4.5-litre (18-cup) slow cooker. Cook, covered, on low, for 8 hours.
3 Carefully remove chicken from cooker. Strain broth through a fine sieve into a large heatproof bowl; discard solids. Skim and discard any fat from broth.
4 Return broth to cooker; add risoni and finely chopped tomatoes. Cook, covered, on high, for 30 minutes or until risoni is tender.
5 Meanwhile, when cool enough to handle, remove meat from bones; discard bones. Shred chicken meat coarsely; add chicken, herbs and juice to soup. Cook, covered, on high, for 5 minutes; season to taste.

nutritional count per serving 14.1g total fat (4.4g saturated fat); 1555kJ (372 cal); 21.7g carbohydrate; 37g protein; 4.5g fibre

notes Recipe not suitable to freeze. Also known as risi, risoni is a small, rice-shaped pasta similar to orzo (which is slightly larger).

GRUYÈRE CROÛTONS

prep + cook time 10 minutes **serves** 4

Preheat grill (broiler). Cut a small french bread stick (150g) into thick slices; discard end pieces of bread stick. Toast slices on one side under grill. Turn slices over and sprinkle tops with equal amounts of cheese; grill croûtons until cheese browns lightly.

GARLIC CROÛTONS

prep + cook time 20 minutes **serves** 4

Preheat oven to 200°C/400°F. Cut 250g (8-ounce) piece ciabatta bread into 2cm (¾-inch) cubes; combine with ¼ cup olive oil and 3 crushed garlic cloves in a large bowl. Place bread, in a single layer, on an oven tray; toast, in oven, turning occasionally, for 20 minutes or until browned lightly and crisp.

PARMESAN CHEESE CROÛTONS

prep + cook time 25 minutes **serves** 6

Preheat grill (broiler). Cut a small french bread stick (150g) into thick slices; discard end pieces of bread stick. Toast slices on one side under grill. Turn slices over and sprinkle tops with ½ cup coarsely grated parmesan. Grill croûtons until cheese browns lightly.

GARLIC AND CHIVE CROÛTONS

prep + cook time 10 minutes **serves** 6

Preheat oven to 180°C/350°F. Cut 150g (4½oz) piece ciabatta into 2cm (¾-inch) cubes; combine bread in a large bowl with 2 tablespoons olive oil, 1 crushed garlic clove and 1 tablespoon finely chopped fresh chives. Place bread, in a single layer, on an oven tray; toast, in oven, turning occasionally, for 12 minutes or until browned lightly and crisp.

123

BEEF

CREAMY SEMI-DRIED TOMATO & VEAL SOUP

prep + cook time 2½ hours (+ cooling) **serves** 6

500g (1-pound) piece boneless veal shoulder
1 litre (4 cups) water
6 black peppercorns
1 dried bay leaf
60g (2 ounces) butter
1 medium brown onion (150g),
   chopped coarsely
1 clove garlic, crushed
⅓ cup (50g) plain (all-purpose) flour
6 large roma (egg) tomatoes (540g),
   chopped coarsely
2 tablespoons tomato paste
½ cup (125ml) pouring cream
⅓ cup (75g) drained semi-dried tomatoes,
   chopped finely
2 tablespoons finely shredded fresh basil

TOASTED CIABATTA WITH BASIL BUTTER
50g (1½ ounces) butter, softened
1 tablespoon finely chopped fresh basil
8 thick slices ciabatta (280g)

1 Place veal in a large saucepan with the water, peppercorns and bay leaf; bring to the boil. Reduce heat; simmer, covered, for 1½ hours or until veal is tender.
2 Transfer veal to a medium bowl; using two forks, shred veal coarsely. Strain broth through a muslin-lined sieve or colander into a large heatproof bowl; discard solids.
3 Melt butter in a large saucepan over medium heat; cook onion and garlic, stirring, until onion softens. Add flour; cook, stirring, until mixture thickens and bubbles. Gradually stir in broth; stir over medium heat until soup boils and thickens slightly. Add fresh tomato and paste; return to the boil. Reduce heat; simmer, covered, 10 minutes. Cool 15 minutes.
4 Meanwhile, make toasted ciabatta with basil butter.
5 Blend or process soup, in batches, until smooth. Return soup to pan, add cream; stir over medium heat until hot. Season to taste.
6 Serve soup topped with shredded veal, semi-dried tomato and basil; accompany with toasted ciabatta.

TOASTED CIABATTA WITH BASIL BUTTER
Combine butter and basil in a small bowl. Toast ciabatta on both sides; spread with basil butter.

nutritional count per serving 28.2g total fat (16.6g saturated fat); 2090kJ (500 cal); 33g carbohydrate; 26.3g protein; 5.4g fibre

notes Recipe can be frozen at the end of step 3. Thaw overnight in the fridge. Reheat in a large saucepan, then continue from step 4.

LENTIL AND PAPRIKA MEATBALL MINESTRONE

prep + cook time 35 minutes **serves** 4

200g (4 ounces) lean minced (ground) beef
1 teaspoon smoked paprika
1 teaspoon ground cumin
cooking-oil spray
1 medium brown onion (150g),
   chopped finely
1 medium carrot (120g), chopped finely
2 trimmed stalks celery (200g),
   chopped finely
1 medium zucchini (120g), chopped finely
2 x 400g (12½ ounces) cans diced tomatoes
1 litre (4 cups) chicken stock
⅔ cup (130g) french-style lentils

GREMOLATA
2 cloves garlic, sliced thinly
2 tablespoons fresh flat-leaf parsley leaves
4 teaspoons finely grated lemon rind

1 Combine mince, paprika and cumin in a small bowl. Roll teaspoons of mixture into balls. Lightly spray a large saucepan with oil; cook meatballs, over high heat, turning occasionally, for 2 minutes or until golden. Transfer to a bowl.

2 Add onion, carrot, celery and zucchini to same pan; cook, stirring, for 4 minutes or until onion softens. Add tomato, stock, lentils and meatballs; bring to the boil. Reduce heat to medium; cook, covered, for 20 minutes or until lentils are tender. Season to taste.

3 Meanwhile, make gremolata; sprinkle over minestrone to serve.

GREMOLATA Preheat grill (broiler). Line an oven tray with paper. Place garlic on tray; gently grill for 2 minutes or until golden on both sides. Combine with parsley and lemon.

nutritional count per serving 8.2g total fat; 2.4g saturated fat; 1253kJ (299 cal); 26.1g carbohydrate; 25.4g protein; 11.6g fibre

notes Recipe is suitable to freeze without the gremolata. Thaw overnight in the fridge. Reheat in a large saucepan, then continue from step 3.

PHO BO

prep + cook time 3 hours serves 6

This is Vietnam's famous beef noodle soup.

1.5kg (3 pounds) beef bones
2 medium brown onions (300g),
    chopped coarsely
2 medium carrots (240g), chopped coarsely
4 stalks celery (600g), trimmed,
    chopped coarsely
2 cinnamon sticks
4 star anise
6 cardamom pods, bruised
10 black peppercorns
2 tablespoons fish sauce
6 cloves
12cm (4¾-inch) piece fresh ginger (60g),
    sliced thinly
6 cloves garlic, sliced thinly
500g (1-pound) piece gravy beef
4 litres (16 cups) water
2 tablespoons light soy sauce
200g (6½ ounces) bean thread vermicelli
½ cup loosely packed fresh
    vietnamese mint leaves
4 fresh small red thai (serrano) chillies,
    sliced thinly
1 medium brown onion (150g), extra,
    sliced thinly
½ cup loosely packed fresh coriander leaves
    (cilantro)
1¼ cups (100g) bean sprouts

1 Preheat oven to 220°C/425°F.
2 Combine beef bones, onion, carrot and celery in a large baking dish; roast, uncovered, about 45 minutes or until browned all over. Drain excess fat from dish.
3 Combine beef mixture, cinnamon, star anise, cardamom, peppercorns, fish sauce, cloves, ginger, garlic, gravy beef and the water a in large saucepan; bring to the boil. Reduce heat; simmer, uncovered, 1½ hours, skimming occasionally. Strain through a muslin-lined sieve or colander into a large heatproof bowl. Reserve broth and beef; discard solids.
4 When beef is cool enough to handle, shred meat finely. Return beef to cleaned pan with soy sauce and broth; bring to the boil. Season to taste.
5 Just before serving, place vermicelli in a large heatproof bowl; cover with boiling water. Stand for 3 minutes; separate with a fork, drain.
6 Divide vermicelli among serving bowls; top with broth and beef mixture, mint, chilli, extra onion and coriander. Serve with sprouts.

nutritional count per serving 4.7g total fat (1.9g saturated fat); 1074kJ (257 cal); 30.1g carbohydrate; 23g protein; 6.2g fibre

notes Recipe is not suitable to freeze. This soup can also be served with the beef raw, so diners can drop it into the hot broth to cook.

CHUNKY BEEF & VEGETABLE SOUP

prep + cook time 2½ hours **serves** 4

2 tablespoons olive oil

600g (1¼ pounds) gravy beef, trimmed,
   cut into 2cm (¾ inch) pieces

1 medium brown onion (150g),
   chopped coarsely

1 clove garlic, crushed

1.5 litres (6 cups) water

1 cup (250ml) beef stock

400g (12½ ounces) canned diced tomatoes

2 stalks celery (300g), trimmed, cut into
   1cm (½-inch) pieces

1 medium carrot (120g), cut into
   1cm (½-inch) pieces

2 small potatoes (240g), cut into
   1cm (½-inch) pieces

310g (10 ounces) canned corn kernels,
   rinsed, drained

½ cup (60g) frozen peas

1 Heat half the oil in a large saucepan over medium-high heat; cook beef, in batches, until browned. Remove from pan.

2 Heat remaining oil in same pan over medium heat; cook onion and garlic, stirring, until onion softens. Return beef to pan with the water, stock and tomatoes; bring to the boil. Reduce heat; simmer, covered, for 1½ hours.

3 Add celery, carrot and potato to soup; simmer, uncovered, about 20 minutes or until vegetables are tender.

4 Add corn and peas to soup; stir over heat until peas are tender. Season to taste.

nutritional count per serving 17g total fat (4.3g saturated fat); 1768kJ (423 cal); 26.7g carbohydrate; 36.9g protein; 7.5g fibre

notes Recipe is suitable to freeze.
For an added vegie kick, trim and coarsely chop a bunch of spinach and add with the corn and peas.

SLOW COOKER BORSCHT

prep + cook time 9 hours **serves** 6

60g (2 ounces) butter
2 medium brown onions (300g),
   chopped finely
500g (1 pound) beef chuck steak, cut
   into large chunks
1 cup (250ml) water
750g (1½ pounds) beetroot (beets),
   chopped finely
2 medium potatoes (400g), chopped finely
2 medium carrots (240g), chopped finely
4 small tomatoes (360g), chopped finely
1 litre (4 cups) beef stock
⅓ cup (80ml) red wine vinegar
3 dried bay leaves
4 cups (320g) finely shredded cabbage
2 tablespoons coarsely chopped fresh
   flat-leaf parsley
½ cup (120g) sour cream

1 Melt half the butter in a large frying pan over medium heat; cook onion, stirring, until soft. Transfer onion to a 4.5-litre (18-cup) slow cooker.

2 Melt remaining butter in same pan over medium-high heat; cook beef, stirring, until browned all over. Transfer beef to slow cooker. Add the water to same frying pan; bring to the boil, then add to slow cooker with beetroot, potato, carrot, tomato, stock, vinegar and bay leaves. Cook, covered, on low, 8 hours.

3 Discard bay leaves. Remove beef from soup; shred using two forks. Return beef to soup.

4 Stir cabbage into soup; cook, covered, on high, about 20 minutes or until wilted. Stir in parsley. Season to taste.

5 Serve soup topped with sour cream.

nutritional count per serving 20.6g total fat (12.4g saturated fat); 1689kJ (404 cal); 25.3g carbohydrate; 25.3g protein; 8.8g fibre

notes Recipe is suitable to freeze at the end of step 3. Thaw overnight in the refrigerator; reheat then continue from step 4.

BEEF & BARLEY SOUP

prep + cook time 2¼ hours **serves** 6

1 tablespoon olive oil

500g (1 pound) gravy beef, trimmed,
   cut into 2.5cm (1-inch) pieces

2 cloves garlic, crushed

2 medium brown onions (300g),
   chopped finely

¾ cup (150g) pearl barley

3 cups (750ml) beef stock

1.5 litres (6 cups) water

1 dried bay leaf

1 sprig fresh thyme

1 sprig fresh rosemary

2 medium potatoes (400g), cut into
   1cm (½-inch) pieces

2 medium carrots (240g), cut into
   1cm (½-inch) pieces

2 medium zucchini (240g), cut into
   1cm (½-inch) pieces

2 medium yellow patty-pan squash (60g),
   cut into 1cm (½-inch) pieces

100g (3 ounces) swiss brown mushrooms,
   chopped coarsely

½ cup finely chopped fresh flat-leaf parsley

1 Heat half the oil in a large saucepan over medium-high heat; cook beef, in batches, until browned. Remove from pan.

2 Heat remaining oil in the same pan; cook garlic and onion, stirring, until onion softens. Return beef to pan with barley, stock, the water, bay leaf, thyme and rosemary; bring to the boil. Reduce heat; simmer, covered, for 1 hour or until beef and barley are tender, skimming fat occasionally.

3 Add potato, carrot, zucchini, squash and mushrooms to soup; simmer, covered, for 25 minutes or until vegetables are tender. Discard bay leaf, thyme and rosemary. Season to taste.

4 Serve soup sprinkled with parsley.

---

nutritional count per serving 8.8g total fat (2.6g saturated fat); 1350kJ (323 cal); 30g carbohydrate; 26.9g protein; 7.8g fibre

notes Recipe is suitable to freeze at the end of step 2. Thaw soup overnight in the fridge. Reheat in a saucepan, then start from step 3.

BEEF DUMPLING SOUP

prep + cook time 40 minutes **serves** 4

1.5 litres (6 cups) water
2 cups (500ml) beef stock
10cm (4-inch) stick lemon grass (20g),
  halved lengthways
2 fresh kaffir lime leaves
1 tablespoon light soy sauce
1 tablespoon lime juice
500g (1 pound) baby buk choy,
  chopped coarsely
1 cup (80g) bean sprouts
¼ cup loosely packed fresh coriander leaves
  (cilantro)
1 fresh small red thai (serrano) chilli,
  sliced finely

BEEF DUMPLINGS
185g (6 ounces) minced (ground) beef
2.5cm (1-inch) piece fresh ginger (10g),
  grated coarsely
1 clove garlic, crushed
1 tablespoon finely chopped fresh coriander
  (cilantro)
1 tablespoon light soy sauce
1 fresh small red thai (serrano) chilli,
  chopped finely
20 gow gee wrappers

1 Make beef dumplings.
2 Combine the water, stock, lemon grass and lime leaves in a large saucepan; bring to the boil. Reduce heat; simmer broth, uncovered, 15 minutes. Discard lemon grass and leaves.
3 Return broth to the boil; add dumplings. Simmer, uncovered, 5 minutes or until dumplings are cooked through. Stir in soy sauce and lime juice. Season to taste.
4 Divide buk choy between bowls; ladle hot broth and dumplings over the top. Serve with bean sprouts, coriander and chilli.

BEEF DUMPLINGS Combine mince, ginger, garlic, coriander, sauce and chilli in a medium bowl. Place rounded teaspoons of mince mixture in the centre of each gow gee wrapper. Brush edges with water; pinch points of wrappers together to completely enclose filling and seal.

nutritional count per serving 5.4g total fat (2.1g saturated fat); 1062kJ (254 cal); 31g carbohydrate; 18g protein; 3.7g fibre

notes Broth and uncooked dumplings can be frozen, separately, for up to 3 months; dumplings can be cooked in the broth from frozen.

FRENCH ONION SOUP

prep + cook time 45 minutes serves 4

This may be a simple soup, but it is full of robust flavours – a homemade beef stock will lift it to another level. Make sure the onions are fully caramelised before adding the wine.

80g (2½ ounces) butter
6 large brown onions (1.2kg), sliced thinly
2 tablespoons finely chopped fresh thyme
⅔ cup (160ml) dry white wine
2 tablespoons plain (all-purpose) flour
1½ litres (6 cups) salt-reduced beef stock
2 cups (500ml) water
1 small french bread stick (50g), ends
   trimmed, cut into 4 slices
½ cup (60g) finely grated gruyère cheese

1 Melt butter in a large saucepan over medium heat; cook onion and thyme, stirring, for about 20 minutes or until onion is caramelised. Add wine; bring to the boil. Add flour; cook, stirring, until mixture bubbles and thickens.
2 Gradually add stock and the water to pan; cook, stirring, until mixture boils and thickens. Reduce heat; simmer, uncovered, for 15 minutes. Season to taste.
3 Meanwhile, preheat grill (broiler). Place bread on an oven tray; grill until browned lightly each side. Sprinkle cheese over one side of each toast; grill until cheese melts.
4 Serve soup topped with cheese toasts.

nutritional count per serving 7.5g total fat (4.4g saturated fat); 1421kJ (340 cal); 36.6g carbohydrate; 22.1g protein; 4.9g fibre

notes Recipe is suitable to freeze.
Thaw overnight in the fridge; reheat in a microwave oven on HIGH (100%) for about 1½ minutes.

BEEF TIPS

SLOW-COOKED OR PRESSURE-COOKED BEEF SOUPS ARE GREAT BECAUSE YOU CAN USE THE TOUGHER, THOUGH CHEAPER, CUTS OF MEAT, SUCH AS GRAVY BEEF, SKIRT AND CHUCK STEAK,

AND BRISKET. THESE CUTS WILL PRODUCE A TENDER, MELT-IN-THE-MOUTH RESULT WHEN SLOW COOKED. FAST-COOKING ASIAN SOUPS GENERALLY REQUIRE TENDER CUTS, SUCH AS BEEF FILLET OR RUMP.

PRESSURE COOKER BEEF & SILVER BEET SOUP

prep + cook time 45 minutes **serves** 8

1 tablespoon olive oil

1 medium brown onion (150g), chopped finely

2 cloves garlic, crushed

2 tablespoons tomato paste

¼ cup (60ml) dry red wine

1 litre (4 cups) water

410g (13 ounces) canned crushed tomatoes

500g (1 pound) piece beef skirt steak

2 dried bay leaves

3 medium silver beet (swiss chard) leaves (240g), trimmed, shredded coarsely

1 Heat oil in a 6-litre (24-cup) pressure cooker; cook onion and garlic, stirring, until onion softens. Add paste; cook, stirring, 2 minutes. Add wine; simmer, uncovered, until liquid reduces by half. Add the water, tomatoes, beef and bay leaves; secure lid. Bring cooker to high pressure according to manufacturer's instructions. Reduce heat to stabilise pressure; cook 25 minutes.

2 Release the steam pressure according to the manufacturer's instructions; remove lid. Discard bay leaves. Remove beef; when cool enough to handle, cut beef in half. Shred beef using two forks.

3 Return beef to soup with silver beet; simmer, uncovered, until silver beet wilts. Season to taste.

nutritional count per serving 4g total fat (1g saturated fat); 506kJ (121 cal); 3.6g carbohydrate; 15.4g protein; 2g fibre

notes Recipe is suitable to freeze before adding the silver beet. Always check the manufacturer's instructions before using a pressure cooker.

SOUPE AU PISTOU WITH VEAL

prep + cook time 2 hours (+ standing) **serves** 8

1 cup (200g) dried cannellini beans
⅓ cup (80ml) olive oil
2 veal shanks (1.5kg), trimmed
1 large leek (500g), sliced thinly
2 litres (8 cups) water
2 cups (500ml) chicken stock
2 tablespoons roasted pine nuts
1 clove garlic, quartered
¼ cup (20g) finely grated parmesan
½ cup firmly packed fresh basil leaves
2 medium carrots (240g), chopped coarsely
200g (6½ ounces) green beans, trimmed,
   chopped coarsely

1 Cover cannellini beans with cold water in a large bowl, cover, stand overnight; drain. Rinse under cold water; drain.

2 Heat 1 tablespoon of the oil in a large saucepan over medium-high heat; cook veal, turning, until browned all over. Remove from pan. Cook leek in same pan, stirring, about 5 minutes or until softened. Return veal to pan with the water and stock; bring to the boil. Reduce heat; simmer, covered, 1 hour or until veal is tender.

3 Meanwhile, blend or process remaining oil, nuts, garlic and cheese until combined. Add basil; process until pistou mixture forms a paste.

4 Remove veal from soup. When cool enough to handle, remove meat from bones. Discard bones; chop meat coarsely. Return meat to soup with beans; bring to the boil. Reduce heat; simmer, uncovered, for 20 minutes or until beans are just tender. Add carrot; simmer, uncovered, 10 minutes. Add green beans and pistou; simmer, uncovered, for 5 minutes. Season to taste.

5 Divide soup into serving bowls; accompany with slices of warm french bread, if you like.

nutritional count per serving 13.5g total fat (2.2g saturated fat); 1210kJ (289 cal); 11.7g carbohydrate; 27.8g protein; 6.9g fibre

notes Recipe is suitable to freeze. Not dissimilar to Italian minestrone, this soup benefits from being made a day in advance.

146

SPICED BEEF AND COCONUT CREAM SOUP WITH RICE

prep + cook time 2 hours **serves** 4

You need to cook ⅔ cup (130g) raw rice to get the amount of cooked rice used here. You could also use microwavable rice, if you prefer.

1 tablespoon vegetable oil
½ large brown onion (100g), chopped finely
1 stalk celery (150g), trimmed,
  chopped finely
2 cloves garlic, chopped finely
1 fresh long red chilli, chopped finely
1 fresh small red thai (serrano) chilli,
  chopped finely
6cm (2½ inch) piece fresh ginger (30g),
  sliced thickly
3 teaspoons tamarind paste (concentrate)
1½ teaspoons each ground turmeric
  and ginger
450g (14½ ounces) beef chuck steak
2 cups (500ml) canned coconut milk
2 cups (500ml) water or beef stock
1 cinnamon stick
4 cardamom pods
⅓ cup (25g) moist coconut flakes
100g (3 ounces) green beans,
  chopped coarsely
2 cups (300g) cooked long-grain white rice
⅓ cup fresh coriander (cilantro) leaves

1 Heat oil in a large saucepan over medium heat; add onion, celery, garlic, chillies, ginger, tamarind and ground spices. Cook, stirring, until vegetables are softened.
2 Cut beef into 4cm (1½-inch) pieces. Increase heat to high, add beef to pan; cook, stirring, until browned. Add coconut milk, the water, cinnamon and cardamom. Bring to the boil; reduce heat, simmer, covered, about 1½ hours or until beef is very tender.
3 Meanwhile, toast coconut in a small dry frying pan until browned lightly; remove from pan.
4 Remove beef from soup. Discard cinnamon and cardamom. Shred beef; return to soup with beans. Simmer for 5 minutes or until beans are tender.
5 Add rice to soup; stir soup over medium heat until hot. Season to taste.
6 Serve soup sprinkled with coriander and toasted coconut.

nutritional count per serving 40.1g total fat 29.1g saturated fat; 2499kJ (597 cal); 29.4g carbohydrate; 28.6g protein; 6.2g fibre

notes Recipe is not suitable to freeze. Tamarind paste is a purple-black, sour paste. It is available from larger supermarkets.

BEEFY BLACK-EYED BEAN & SPINACH SOUP

prep + cook time 2 hours (+ standing) serves 4

1 cup (200g) black-eyed beans
1 tablespoon olive oil
1 medium brown onion (150g),
   chopped finely
1 clove garlic, crushed
2.5 litres (10 cups) beef stock
¼ cup (60ml) dry red wine
2 tablespoons tomato paste
500g (1-pound) piece beef skirt steak
250g (8 ounces) trimmed spinach,
   chopped coarsely

1 Place beans in a medium bowl, cover with water, stand overnight; drain. Rinse under cold water; drain.

2 Heat oil in a large saucepan over medium heat; cook onion and garlic, stirring, until onion softens. Add stock, wine, paste and beef to pan; bring to the boil. Reduce heat; simmer, covered, for 40 minutes. Uncover; simmer for a further 30 minutes.

3 Remove beef from pan. Add beans to pan; bring to the boil. Reduce heat; simmer, uncovered, until beans are tender.

4 Meanwhile, when beef is cool enough to handle, remove and discard fat and sinew. Chop beef coarsely, return to pan with spinach; simmer, uncovered, until soup is hot. Season to taste.

nutritional count per serving 13.9g total fat (4.2g saturated fat); 2199kJ (526 cal); 28.3g carbohydrate; 62.6g protein; 12.4g fibre

notes Recipe is suitable to freeze before adding the spinach. Thaw overnight in the fridge; reheat until hot then add spinach as per step 4.

HUNGARIAN GOULASH

prep + cook time 2½ hours serves 4

Spätzle, served throughout Austria, Germany, Switzerland and the French region of Alsace, are tiny noodle-like dumplings made by pushing a batter through the holes of a colander into a pan of boiling water or stock.

2 tablespoons olive oil
40g (1½ ounces) butter
900g (1¾ pounds) boneless veal shoulder, chopped coarsely
2 medium brown onions (300g), chopped finely
1 tablespoon tomato paste
1 tablespoon plain (all-purpose) flour
1 tablespoon sweet paprika
2 teaspoons caraway seeds
½ teaspoon cayenne pepper
2 cloves garlic, crushed
2 cups (500ml) water
1.5 litres (6 cups) beef stock
400g (12½ ounces) canned crushed tomatoes
1 large red capsicum (bell pepper) (350g), chopped coarsely
1 medium potato (200g), chopped coarsely

SPÄTZLE
1 cup (150g) plain (all-purpose) flour
2 eggs, beaten lightly
¼ cup (60ml) water
½ teaspoon cracked black pepper

1 Heat half the oil and half the butter in a large saucepan over medium-high heat; cook veal, in batches, until browned all over. Remove from pan.
2 Heat remaining oil and remaining butter in same pan over medium heat; cook onion, stirring, about 5 minutes or until onion is slightly caramelised.
3 Add paste, flour, paprika, seeds, cayenne and garlic to pan; cook, stirring, 2 minutes. Return veal to pan with the water, stock and tomatoes; bring to the boil. Reduce heat; simmer, uncovered, 1½ hours. Add capsicum and potato; simmer, uncovered, for about 10 minutes or until potato is tender. Season to taste.
4 Make spätzle; drop onto top of soup.

SPÄTZLE Place flour in a small bowl, make a well in the centre. Gradually add combined egg and the water, stirring, until batter is smooth; stir in pepper. Pour batter into a metal colander set over a large saucepan of boiling water. Using a wooden spoon, push batter through holes of colander. Bring water back to the boil; boil, uncovered, 2 minutes or until spätzle float to the surface. Use a slotted spoon to remove spätzle; drain before adding to goulash.

nutritional count per serving 27.3g total fat (9.5g saturated fat); 3022kJ (723 cal); 48g carbohydrate; 68.8g protein; 5.8g fibre

notes Soup is suitable to freeze at the end of step 3. Thaw in fridge overnight; reheat until hot. Cook spätzle just before serving soup.

HEARTY WINTER SOUP

prep + cook time 2½ hours **serves** 4

2 tablespoons olive oil

1kg (2 pounds) gravy beef, trimmed, cut into 2cm (¾-inch) pieces

12 shallots (300g), halved

2 cloves garlic, crushed

2 small parsnips (240g), chopped coarsely

2 small turnips (300g), chopped coarsely

2 medium swedes (rutabaga) (450g), chopped coarsely

300g (10-ounce) piece pumpkin, chopped coarsely

1 cup (250ml) dry white wine

3 cups (750ml) beef stock

3 cups (750ml) water

1 tablespoon tomato paste

4 sprigs fresh thyme

⅓ cup (40g) short-cut vermicelli noodles

1 Heat half the oil in a large saucepan over medium-high heat; cook beef, in batches, until browned. Remove from pan.

2 Heat remaining oil in same pan over medium heat; cook shallot and garlic, stirring, until shallot softens.

3 Return beef to pan with vegetables, wine, stock, the water, paste and thyme; bring to the boil. Reduce heat; simmer, covered, 1½ hours or until beef is tender, stirring occasionally. Season to taste.

4 Add noodles to pan; simmer, uncovered, about 10 minutes or until just softened.

nutritional count per serving 21.4g total fat (6.5g saturated fat); 2387kJ (571 cal); 22g carbohydrate; 58.5g protein; 7.6g fibre

notes Recipe is not suitable to freeze. You can use any cut of stewing steak you like, as these are especially good for long slow cooking.

WATER SPINACH AND BEEF SOUP

prep + cook time 30 minutes (+ refrigeration) **serves** 6

Chinese water spinach is a mild, versatile vegetable with crunchy white stalks and tender, dark green leaves. It resembles a bunch of spinach (which can be substituted) but has longer, more flexible leaves and thicker stems.

500g (1 pound) beef fillet, sliced thinly
2 cloves garlic, crushed
3 green onions (scallions), sliced thinly
2 teaspoons fish sauce
1 teaspoon caster (superfine) sugar
1 fresh small red thai (serrano) chilli, chopped finely
2cm (¾-inch) piece fresh galangal (10g), grated
500g (1 pound) chinese water spinach
1.5 litres (6 cups) water
2 tablespoons lemon juice
¼ cup loosely packed torn fresh vietnamese mint leaves

1 Combine beef, garlic, onion, sauce, sugar, chilli and galangal in a large bowl, cover; refrigerate 3 hours or overnight.
2 Trim spinach stems; crush stems with a meat mallet or rolling pin. Chop leaves coarsely.
3 Bring the water to the boil in a large saucepan, add spinach and beef mixture; simmer, uncovered, 2 minutes.
4 Remove soup from heat; stir in juice and vietnamese mint leaves; season to taste.

nutritional count per serving 4.5g total fat (1.8g saturated fat); 583kJ (139 cal); 2.4g carbohydrate; 20.3g protein; 3g fibre

notes Recipe is not suitable to freeze. For a fuller flavoured soup, marinate the beef overnight and make the soup close to serving.

157

SPICED YOGHURT

prep + cook time 10 minutes **serves** 6

Dry-fry 1 teaspoon each of ground coriander and cumin and ½ teaspoon hot paprika in a non-stick frying pan until fragrant. Combine spices in a small bowl with 1 cup yoghurt and ¼ cup finely chopped fresh mint.

CINNAMON CREAM

prep + cook time 10 minutes **serves** 6

Lightly whisk ½ cup thickened (heavy) cream with an electric mixer until soft peaks form; sprinkle a little ground cinnamon over cream to taste. Top serving cups or soup bowls with a spoonful of cream or place in the refrigerator, covered, until needed.

DILL CREAM

prep + cook time 10 minutes **serves** 6

Combine ½ cup sour cream with 1 tablespoon finely chopped fresh dill in a small bowl. Place dollops of dill cream on top of soup or place in the refrigerator, covered, until needed. Sprinkle extra chopped dill over the bowl of dill cream just before serving.

PAPRIKA BUTTER

prep + cook time 10 minutes **serves** 6

Melt 60g (2oz) butter in a small frying pan; add 2 teaspoons hot paprika. Cook, stirring, for 2 minutes. Remove from heat; stir in 2 finely chopped green onions (scallions). Drizzle over top of soup; serve immediately. The butter goes well with beef or lamb soup.

LAMB

HARIRA WITH LAMB

prep + cook time 2¾ hours (+ standing) **serves** 8

1 cup (200g) dried chickpeas
  (garbanzo beans)
20g (¾ ounce) butter
2 medium brown onions (300g),
  chopped finely
2 stalks celery (300g), trimmed,
  chopped finely
2 cloves garlic, crushed
4cm (1½-inch) piece fresh ginger (20g),
  grated coarsely
1 teaspoon ground cinnamon
½ teaspoon ground black pepper
pinch saffron threads
500g (1 pound) diced lamb
3 large tomatoes (660g), seeded,
  chopped coarsely
2 litres (8 cups) hot water
½ cup (100g) brown lentils
2 tablespoons plain (all-purpose) flour
½ cup (100g) cooked white long-grain rice
½ cup firmly packed fresh coriander leaves
  (cilantro)
2 tablespoons lemon juice

1 Place chickpeas in a medium bowl, cover with water, stand overnight; drain. Rinse under cold water; drain.

2 Melt butter in a large saucepan over medium heat; cook onion, celery and garlic, stirring, until onion softens. Add ginger, cinnamon, pepper and saffron; cook, stirring, until fragrant.

3 Add lamb to pan; cook, stirring, 5 minutes or until lamb is browned. Add chickpeas and tomato; cook, stirring, about 5 minutes or until tomato softens.

4 Stir the water into soup mixture; bring to the boil. Reduce heat; simmer, covered, 45 minutes. Add lentils; simmer, covered, for 1 hour.

5 Blend flour with ½ cup of slightly cooled broth in a small bowl; return to pan with rice. Cook, stirring, until soup comes to the boil and thickens slightly. Remove from heat; stir in coriander and juice. Season to taste.

---

nutritional count per serving 8.6g total fat (4g saturated fat); 1095kJ (262 cal); 23.6g carbohydrate; 20.1g protein; 4.8g fibre

notes Recipe is not suitable to freeze. If you'd prefer a vegetarian option of this soup, see page 303. Microwave rice is fine to use here.

SLOW COOKER VEGETABLE & LAMB SHANK SOUP

prep + cook time 10½ hours **serves** 6

1 tablespoon olive oil
4 french-trimmed lamb shanks (800g)
1 medium brown onion (150g),
   chopped coarsely
2 baby fennel bulbs (260g), sliced thinly
2 medium carrots (240g), chopped coarsely
4 cloves garlic, crushed
2 fresh small red thai (serrano) chillies,
   chopped finely
2 teaspoons each ground cumin
   and coriander
1 teaspoon each ground cinnamon
   and caraway seeds
pinch saffron threads
1.5 litres (6 cups) water
2 cups (500ml) beef stock
400g (12½ ounces) canned diced tomatoes
400g (12½ ounces) canned chickpeas
   (garbanzo beans), rinsed, drained
¾ cup (90g) frozen baby peas
1 cup loosely packed fresh coriander leaves
   (cilantro)

1 Heat half the oil in a large frying pan over medium-high heat; cook lamb until browned all over, then place in a 4.5-litre (18-cup) slow cooker.

2 Heat remaining oil in the same pan over medium heat; cook onion, fennel, carrot, garlic and chilli, stirring, until onion softens. Add spices; cook, stirring, until fragrant. Place vegetable mixture into cooker. Stir in the water, stock, tomatoes and chickpeas. Cook, covered, on low, for 10 hours.

3 Remove lamb from cooker. When cool enough to handle, remove meat from bones, shred meat; discard bones. Stir meat, peas and coriander leaves into cooker. Season to taste.

4 Divide soup into serving bowls; accompany soup with greek-style yoghurt, lemon wedges and crusty bread, if you like.

nutritional count per serving 11.4g total fat (3.7g saturated fat); 1098kJ (262 cal); 15.2g carbohydrate; 21.5g protein; 6.9g fibre

notes Recipe is suitable to freeze at the end of step 3; shred lamb and stir into mixture. Thaw overnight in fridge. Reheat; add peas and coriander.

SCOTCH BROTH

prep + cook time 2¼ hours **serves** 4

1kg (2 pounds) lamb neck chops
¾ cup (150g) pearl barley
2.25 litres (9 cups) water
1 large brown onion (200g), cut into
   1cm (½-inch) pieces
2 medium carrots (240g), cut into
   1cm (½-inch) pieces
1 medium leek (350g), sliced thinly
2 cups (160g) finely shredded cabbage
½ cup coarsely chopped fresh
   flat-leaf parsley

1 Place lamb, barley and the water in a large saucepan; bring to the boil. Reduce heat; simmer, covered, 1 hour, skimming fat from surface occasionally. Add onion, carrot and leek; simmer, covered, about 30 minutes or until carrot is tender.

2 Remove lamb from pan. When cool enough to handle, remove and discard bones; shred lamb coarsely.

3 Return lamb to soup with cabbage; cook, uncovered, about 10 minutes or until cabbage is just tender.

4 Serve soup sprinkled with parsley.

nutritional count per serving 24.3g total fat (10.7g saturated fat); 2241kJ (535 cal); 31.5g carbohydrate; 42.7g protein; 10.5g fibre

notes Recipe is not suitable to freeze. Pearl barley has had the husk discarded and been hulled and polished, much the same as rice.

167

PRESSURE COOKER LAMB, VEGETABLE & LENTIL SOUP

prep + cook time 40 minutes **serves** 8

2 tablespoons olive oil

3 french-trimmed lamb shanks (750g)

1 medium brown onion (150g),
   chopped finely

2 cloves garlic, crushed

2 medium carrots (240g), chopped coarsely

2 stalks celery (300g), trimmed,
   chopped coarsely

155g (5 ounces) piece of pancetta,
   chopped coarsely

1.25 litres (5 cups) water

½ cup (125ml) dry white wine

⅔ cup (130g) french-style green lentils,
   rinsed, drained

½ cup (60g) frozen peas

1 Heat half the oil in a 6-litre (24-cup) pressure cooker; cook lamb, in batches, until browned. Remove from cooker.

2 Heat remaining oil in cooker; cook onion, garlic, carrot, celery and pancetta, stirring, until vegetables soften. Return lamb to cooker with the water and wine; secure lid. Bring cooker to high pressure according to the manufacturer's instructions. Reduce heat to stabilise pressure; cook 20 minutes.

3 Release the steam pressure according to manufacturer's instructions; remove lid. Add lentils; secure lid. Bring cooker to high pressure according to manufacturer's instructions. Reduce heat to stabilise pressure; cook 10 minutes.

4 Release the steam pressure according to the manufacturer's instructions; remove lid. Remove lamb; when cool enough to handle shred meat coarsely, discard bones. Return lamb to cooker with peas; simmer, uncovered until peas are tender. Season to taste.

nutritional count per serving 10.5g total fat (3g saturated fat); 957kJ (229 cal); 9.5g carbohydrate; 19.6g protein; 4.2g fibre

notes Recipe is suitable to freeze. Always check the manufacturer's instructions before using a pressure cooker.

WHITE BEAN & MERGUEZ SOUP WITH GREMOLATA

prep + cook time 40 minutes **serves** 4

You could substitute fresh chorizo sausages if merguez are unavailable.

1 tablespoon olive oil
1 medium red onion (170g),
   chopped coarsely
2 rindless bacon slices (130g),
   chopped coarsely
2 cloves garlic, crushed
400g (12½ ounces) canned diced tomatoes
1.5 litres (6 cups) chicken stock
6 merguez sausages (480g)
800g (1½ pounds) canned white beans,
   rinsed, drained

GREMOLATA
⅓ cup finely chopped fresh flat-leaf parsley
2 teaspoons finely grated lemon rind
2 cloves garlic, crushed

1 Heat olive oil in a large saucepan over medium heat; cook onion, bacon and garlic, stirring, for 8 minutes or until onion softens and bacon crisps. Add tomatoes and stock; bring to the boil. Reduce heat; simmer, uncovered, 20 minutes, stirring occasionally.
2 Meanwhile, cook sausages in a heated oiled medium fry pan, turning, 8 minutes or until browned and cooked through; slice thinly.
3 Add sausage to soup with beans; stir until soup is hot. Season to taste.
4 Make gremolata. Serve bowls of soup sprinkled with gremolata.

GREMOLATA Combine ingredients in a small bowl.

nutritional count per serving 42.4g total fat (15.6g saturated fat); 2504kJ (599 cal); 14.6g carbohydrate; 38.4g protein; 5.5g fibre

notes Recipe is not suitable to freeze. Merguez, a small lamb sausage seasoned with garlic and hot spices, is available from delis.

LAMB & BARLEY SOUP

prep + cook time 1¾ hours serves 6

1.5kg (3 pounds) french-trimmed
   lamb shanks
3 litres (12 cups) water
¾ cup (150g) pearl barley
1 medium carrot (120g), sliced thinly
1 medium leek (350g), sliced thinly
2 stalks celery (300g), trimmed, sliced thinly
1 tablespoon curry powder
250g (8 ounces) trimmed silver beet
   (swiss chard), chopped coarsely

1 Combine lamb, the water and barley in a large saucepan; bring to the boil. Reduce heat; simmer, uncovered, 1 hour, skimming surface and stirring occasionally. Add carrot, leek and celery; simmer, uncovered, for 10 minutes.

2 Remove lamb from soup mixture. When cool enough to handle, remove meat; chop coarsely. Discard bones and fat.

3 Dry-fry curry powder in a small saucepan, over low heat until fragrant. Return meat to soup with curry powder and silver beet; simmer, uncovered, until silver beet wilts. Season to taste.

nutritional count per serving 13.3g total fat (5.7g saturated fat); 1404kJ (336 cal); 18.9g carbohydrate; 31.8g protein; 6.4g fibre

notes Recipe is suitable to freeze. French-trimmed shanks have the gristle and fat removed and the bones scraped cleaned.

SLOW-COOKED LAMB & WHITE BEAN SOUP

prep + cook time 3½ hours **serves** 4

1 tablespoon olive oil

1.5kg (3 pounds) french-trimmed
lamb shanks

1 large brown onion (200g),
chopped coarsely

2 cloves garlic, quartered

2 medium carrots (240g), chopped coarsely

2 stalks celery (300g), trimmed,
chopped coarsely

2 tablespoons tomato paste

1 cup (250ml) dry red wine

3 litres (12 cups) water

400g (12½ ounces) canned white beans,
rinsed, drained

200g (6½ ounces) char-grilled red capsicums
(bell peppers), drained, chopped finely

90g (3 ounces) baby spinach leaves

1 Heat oil in a large saucepan over medium-high heat; cook lamb, in batches, until browned all over. Remove from pan. Reduce heat to medium; cook onion and garlic in same pan, stirring, until onion softens. Add carrot and celery; cook, stirring, for 2 minutes. Add paste and wine; bring to the boil. Reduce heat; simmer, uncovered, for 5 minutes.

2 Return lamb to pan with the water; bring to the boil. Reduce heat; simmer, uncovered, for 2 hours, skimming fat from the surface of the soup occasionally.

3 Remove lamb from pan. Strain broth through a muslin-lined sieve or colander into a large heatproof bowl; discard solids. When lamb is cool enough to handle, remove meat from shanks; shred coarsely. Discard bones.

4 Return broth to same cleaned pan with beans and lamb; bring to the boil. Reduce heat; simmer, uncovered, 5 minutes or until heated through. Remove from heat.

5 Add capsicum and spinach to soup, stir until spinach is wilted. Season to taste.

---

nutritional count per serving 1.8g total fat
(0.7g saturated fat); 171kJ (41 cal);
1.4g carbohydrate; 3.8g protein; 0.7g fibre

notes Recipe is suitable to freeze at the end of step 4. Thaw overnight in the fridge. Reheat in a large saucepan, then continue from step 5.

LAMB TIPS

LAMB SHANKS ARE A GREAT CUT TO USE IN SOUPS. ITS FLAVOUR IS ENHANCED BY BONE MARROW, FOUND IN THE SHANK, WHICH INFUSES THE SOUP AS IT COOKS. FOR MEAT THAT IS MELTINGLY TENDER

AND SIMPLY FALLS OFF THE BONE, TRY SLOW COOKING LAMB SHOULDER, LEG AND NECK CHOPS. BEANS, LENTILS, RICE, QUINOA OR PEARL BARLEY CAN BE ADDED TO THE SOUP FOR A LITTLE EXTRA FIBRE.

GREEK LAMB &
BUTTER BEAN SOUP

prep + cook time 2½ hours (+ standing) **serves** 8

1 cup (200g) dried butter beans
2 tablespoons olive oil
3 french-trimmed lamb shanks (600g)
2 medium brown onions (300g),
  chopped finely
1 clove garlic, crushed
2 medium carrots (240g), chopped finely
2 stalks celery (300g), trimmed,
  chopped finely
2 cups (500ml) chicken stock
1 litre (4 cups) water
400g (12½ ounces) canned chopped
  tomatoes
¼ cup coarsely chopped fresh dill
2 tablespoons lemon juice

1 Place beans in a medium bowl, cover with water, stand overnight; drain.
2 Heat oil in a large saucepan over medium-high heat; cook lamb, in batches, until browned all over. Remove from pan. Reduce heat to medium, add onion, garlic, carrot and celery to same pan; cook, stirring, until soft.
3 Return lamb to pan with beans, stock and the water; bring to the boil. Reduce heat; simmer, covered, 1 hour, skimming surface occasionally.
4 Remove lamb shanks from pan. When cool enough to handle, remove meat from bones, discard bones; shred meat. Return meat to pan with tomatoes; simmer, covered, 1 hour. Stir in dill and juice. Season to taste.

nutritional count per serving 8.3g total fat (2.1g saturated fat); 928kJ (222 cal); 15.3g carbohydrate; 18.2g protein; 6.8g fibre

note Recipe is suitable to freeze. Butter beans are also known as lima beans. Cannellini or haricot beans may also be used.

LAMB SHANK
& VEGETABLE SOUP

prep + cook time 2 hours **serves** 4

4 french-trimmed lamb shanks (800g)
2 medium white onions (300g),
  chopped coarsely
2 cloves garlic, crushed
2 medium potatoes (400g),
  chopped coarsely
2 medium carrots (240g), chopped coarsely
2 stalks celery (300g), trimmed,
  chopped coarsely
400g (12½ ounces) canned chopped
  tomatoes
1.5 litres (6 cups) beef or chicken stock
½ cup (125ml) tomato paste
2 medium zucchini (240g), chopped coarsely

1 Place lamb, onion, garlic, potato, carrot, celery, tomatoes, stock and paste in a large saucepan; bring to the boil. Reduce heat; simmer, covered, 1 hour.
2 Add zucchini; simmer, uncovered, for a further 30 minutes or until lamb is tender.
3 Remove lamb from soup. When cool enough to handle, remove meat from shanks; discard bones. Return meat to soup; stir over heat until hot. Season to taste.

nutritional count per serving 9.2g total fat (3.9g saturated fat); 1513kJ (362 cal); 29.2g carbohydrate; 39.7g protein; 8.5g fibre

notes Recipe is suitable to freeze. Mixed dried beans, lentils or diced potato will make a nice addition to this hearty soup.

CUBAN LAMB & BLACK BEAN SOUP

prep + cook time 2 hours (+ standing) **serves** 6

Black beans, also known as turtle beans, are a common ingredient in Latin American soups, salads and salsa. They have a black skin, creamy texture and sweet flavour, and are a breed apart from Chinese black beans which are, in fact, fermented soya beans.

2 cups (400g) dried black beans
2 tablespoons olive oil
500g (1 pound) boneless lamb shoulder,
    cut into 1.5cm (¾-inch) pieces
1 large red onion (300g), chopped finely
2 cloves garlic, crushed
2 stalks celery (300g), trimmed, sliced thinly
1 tablespoon ground cumin
½ teaspoon ground cayenne pepper
2.5 litres (10 cups) water
400g (12½ ounces) canned crushed
    tomatoes
¼ cup (60ml) dry sherry
¼ cup (60ml) balsamic vinegar
¼ cup coarsely chopped fresh coriander
    (cilantro)
2 limes
4 fresh small red thai (serrano) chillies,
    seeded, chopped finely
⅓ cup (80ml) white wine vinegar
½ cup (120g) sour cream

1 Place beans in a medium bowl, cover with cold water, stand overnight; drain. Rinse under cold water; drain.
2 Heat half the oil in a large saucepan over medium-high heat; cook lamb, in batches, until browned. Remove from pan.
3 Heat remaining oil in same pan over medium heat; cook onion and garlic, stirring, until onion is soft. Add celery, cumin and cayenne; cook, stirring, until fragrant.
4 Return lamb to pan with the water and tomatoes; bring to the boil. Reduce heat; simmer, covered, 30 minutes. Add beans; simmer, covered, about 1 hour or until beans are tender. Stir in sherry and balsamic vinegar; cool 10 minutes.
5 Blend or process half the soup, in batches, until pureed. [Soup can be made ahead to this stage. Cover; refrigerate overnight.]
6 Combine pureed soup with coriander and remaining soup in pan; stir over heat until hot. Season to taste.
7 Meanwhile, cut limes into wedges. Combine chilli and white wine vinegar in a small bowl. Serve soup accompanied by lime wedges, chilli mixture and sour cream.

nutritional count per serving 20.1g total fat (8.3g saturated fat); 2100kJ (502 cal); 32.7g carbohydrate; 34.7g protein; 18.6g fibre

notes Recipe not suitable to freeze. You can substitute gravy beef (or better yet, a ham bone and chicken stock) for the lamb.

LAMB & BLACK-EYED BEAN SOUP

prep + cook time 3 hours (+ standing) serves 6

2 cups (400g) black-eyed beans
1 tablespoon olive oil
1.5kg (3 pounds) french-trimmed
lamb shanks
1 medium brown onion (150g),
chopped coarsely
2 cloves garlic, quartered
2 medium carrots (240g), chopped coarsely
2 stalks celery (300g), trimmed,
chopped coarsely
400g (12½ ounces) canned crushed
tomatoes
1.750 litres (7 cups) beef stock
1.750 litres (7 cups) water
2 medium red capsicums (bell peppers)
(400g)
1 tablespoon coarsely chopped fresh
coriander (cilantro)

1 Place beans in a medium bowl, cover with cold water, stand overnight; drain. Rinse under cold water; drain.
2 Heat oil in a large saucepan over medium-high heat; cook lamb, in batches, until browned all over. Remove from pan. Reduce heat to medium; cook onion and garlic in same pan, stirring, until onion softens. Add carrot and celery; cook, stirring, 2 minutes.

3 Add tomatoes and stock to pan; bring to the boil. Reduce heat; simmer, uncovered, 5 minutes. Return lamb to pan with the water; bring to the boil. Reduce heat; simmer, uncovered, 1 hour, skimming surface occasionally. Strain through a muslin-lined sieve or colander into a large bowl. Reserve lamb and stock; discard solids. [Soup can be made ahead to this stage. Cover; refrigerate overnight or freeze.]
4 Return lamb and stock to same cleaned pan; add beans, bring to the boil. Reduce heat, simmer for 1 hour or until beans are tender. Remove lamb from stock; cool.
5 Meanwhile, preheat grill (broiler). Quarter capsicums; discard seeds and membranes. Roast under grill, skin-side up, until skin blisters and blackens. Cover capsicum pieces with plastic or paper for 5 minutes; peel away skin, dice capsicum finely.
6 When cool enough to handle, remove meat from lamb bones; discard bones, shred meat coarsely.
7 Return lamb to pan with capsicum; stir over heat until hot. Just before serving soup, stir in coriander. Season to taste. Accompany with warm crusty bread, if you like.

nutritional count per serving 15.9g total fat (6.1g saturated fat); 1616kJ (386 cal); 19.2g carbohydrate; 36.3g protein; 11g fibre

notes Recipe is suitable to freeze at the end of step 3. The bone-coloured black-eye bean has a black speck of an "eye" in the curve of one side.

LAMB SHANK SOUP

prep + cook time 2¾ hours (+ standing & refrigeration) **serves** 4

You need to start this recipe the day before
serving.

1½ cups (300g) dried chickpeas
  (garbanzo beans)
1 tablespoon olive oil
1.5kg (3 pounds) french-trimmed
  lamb shanks
1 medium brown onion (150g),
  chopped finely
2 medium carrots (240g), chopped finely
2 stalks celery (300g), trimmed, sliced thinly
2 cloves garlic, crushed
1 teaspoon ground cumin
2 cups (500ml) chicken stock
1 litre (4 cups) water
8 large stalks silver beet (swiss chard)
  (400g), trimmed, chopped finely
¼ cup (60ml) lemon juice

1 Place chickpeas in a medium bowl, cover
with water, stand overnight; drain. Rinse
under cold water; drain.
2 Meanwhile, heat oil in a large saucepan
over medium-high heat; cook lamb, in
batches, until browned. Remove from pan.
3 Cook onion, carrot, celery, garlic and cumin
in same pan, stirring, for 5 minutes or until
onion softens. Return lamb to pan with stock
and the water; bring to the boil. Reduce heat;
simmer, covered, 2 hours.
4 Remove pan from heat; when lamb is cool
enough to handle, remove meat from bones.
Discard bones; chop meat coarsely. Refrigerate
cooled soup mixture and lamb meat, covered
separately, overnight.
5 Discard fat from surface of soup mixture.
Place soup mixture, meat and chickpeas in
a large saucepan; bring to the boil. Reduce
heat; simmer, covered, 30 minutes.
6 Add silver beet and juice to soup; simmer,
uncovered, until silver beet just wilts. Divide
soup into serving bowls; accompany with a
warmed loaf of ciabatta, if you like.

nutritional count per serving 28.2g total fat
(9.9g saturated fat); 2654kJ (635 cal);
35.7g carbohydrate; 59.1g protein; 15.6g fibre

notes Recipe is suitable to freeze before adding
silver beet. Thaw overnight in the fridge. Reheat
in a saucepan and start from step 6.

SLOW COOKER LAMB & PUMPKIN SOUP

prep + cook time 6½ hours **serves** 4

½ cup (100g) dried brown lentils
3 french-trimmed lamb shanks (600g)
2 tablespoons moroccan seasoning
500g (1 pound) pumpkin, chopped coarsely
1 litre (4 cups) chicken stock
400g (12½ ounces) canned diced tomatoes
400g (12½ ounces) canned chickpeas
   (garbanzo beans), rinsed, drained
½ cup finely chopped fresh flat-leaf parsley

1 Rinse lentils under cold water until water runs clear; drain.
2 Combine lamb, seasoning, pumpkin, stock, tomatoes, chickpeas and lentils in a 4.5-litre (18-cup) slow cooker. Cook, covered, on low, for 6 hours.
3 Remove lamb from cooker. When cool enough to handle, remove meat from bones; shred coarsely. Discard bones. Return meat to cooker; season to taste. Serve sprinkled with parsley.

SERVING SUGGESTION Serve with a dollop of thick yoghurt and crusty bread.

nutritional count per serving 10.6g total fat (4.3g saturated fat); 1614kJ (386 cal); 34.7g carbohydrate; 34.1g protein; 10.3g fibre

notes Recipe is suitable to freeze without the parsley. Thaw overnight in the fridge. Reheat in a saucepan and sprinkle with parsley to serve.

PISTOU

prep + cook time 10 minutes **serves** 6

Blend or process 2 cups loosely packed fresh basil leaves, 1 quartered garlic clove, ¼ cup finely grated parmesan and ¼ cup extra virgin olive oil until smooth. Refrigerate, covered. If storing for a few days, omit the cheese when preparing and stir in just before serving.

TORTILLA CRISPS

prep + cook time 10 minutes **serves** 6

Slice 2 x 15cm (6-inch) soft corn tortillas into thin strips; shallow-fry in vegetable oil, in batches, until browned lightly. Drain on absorbent paper. The crisps go well with tomato soup and Mexican-style soups along with cubes of avocado or a spoonful of chilli con carne.

GREMOLATA

prep + cook time 10 minutes **serves 6**

Combine ⅓ cup finely chopped fresh flat-leaf parsley, 1 tablespoon finely grated lemon rind and 2 cloves finely chopped garlic in a small bowl. Keep covered with plastic wrap or in an airtight container in the fridge until ready to use.

CUCUMBER & ONION SALSA

prep + cook time 10 minutes **serves 6**

Combine ¼ cup sour cream, 1 finely chopped, seeded lebanese cucumber, 1 finely chopped small red onion and 1 finely chopped small red thai (serrano) chilli in a small bowl. Serve on the side with soup, or place in the refrigerator, covered, until ready to serve.

PORK

CREAM OF MUSHROOM AND PANCETTA SOUP

prep + cook time 1½ hours (+ standing & cooling) **serves** 4

10g (½ ounce) dried porcini mushrooms
1 cup (250ml) boiling water
40g (1½ ounces) butter
1 medium brown onion (150g),
    chopped coarsely
1 small leek (200g), sliced thinly
250g (8 ounces) button mushrooms,
    sliced thickly
⅓ cup (80ml) dry white wine
3 cups (750ml) chicken stock
1 large potato (300g), chopped coarsely
300ml pouring cream
2 tablespoons coarsely chopped
    fresh tarragon
6 slices pancetta (90g)

1 Place porcini in a small heatproof bowl, cover with the boiling water; stand for 30 minutes. Drain liquid through fine sieve into small bowl; reserve liquid. Coarsely chop porcini.
2 Meanwhile, melt butter in a large saucepan over medium heat; cook onion and leek, stirring, until vegetables soften. Add button mushrooms; cook, stirring, about 10 minutes or until mushrooms soften and liquid evaporates. Add wine; cook, stirring, about 5 minutes or until liquid reduces by half. Add reserved porcini liquid, stock and potato; bring to the boil. Reduce heat; simmer, uncovered, about 10 minutes or until potato is tender. Remove soup from heat; cool 15 minutes.
3 Blend or process soup, in batches, until smooth. Return soup to pan; bring to the boil. Add cream; reduce heat, stir over medium heat until soup is hot. Remove from heat; stir in tarragon. Season to taste.
4 Meanwhile, cook pancetta in a heated medium frying pan until crisp; drain on absorbent paper.
5 Serve soup with pancetta and sprinkled with porcini.

nutritional count per serving 44.9g total fat (28.4g saturated fat); 2228kJ (533 cal); 15.6g carbohydrate; 13g protein; 4g fibre

notes Recipe is not suitable to freeze. Dried porcini mushrooms are available from larger supermarkets and good greengrocers.

RAMEN, PORK & SPINACH SOUP

prep + cook time 1¾ hours (+ refrigeration) serves 4

1kg (2 pounds) chicken necks
3 litres (12 cups) water
1 large leek (500g), chopped coarsely
5cm (2-inch) piece fresh ginger (25g),
    sliced thinly
10 black peppercorns
250g (8 ounces) fresh ramen noodles
¼ cup (60ml) japanese soy sauce
¼ cup (60ml) cooking sake
1 teaspoon sesame oil
300g (9½ ounces) spinach, trimmed,
    chopped coarsely
200g (6½-ounce) piece chinese barbecued
    pork, sliced thinly
1 fresh long red chilli, sliced thinly
½ sheet nori, cut into 2cm (¾-inch) pieces

1 Combine chicken, the water, leek, ginger and peppercorns in a large saucepan; bring to the boil. Reduce heat; simmer, uncovered, 1 hour. Strain broth through a muslin-lined sieve or colander into a large heatproof bowl; discard solids. Allow broth to cool; cover. Refrigerate until cold.

2 Place noodles in a large heatproof bowl, cover with boiling water; separate with a fork, stand 2 minutes, drain.

3 Skim and discard fat from surface of broth, return broth to cleaned pan; bring to the boil. Stir in sauce, sake and oil; return to the boil. Season to taste.

4 Divide noodles, spinach, pork, chilli and nori into serving bowls; ladle broth into bowls.

nutritional count per serving 12.4g total fat (4.8g saturated fat); 1680kJ (402 cal); 40.1g carbohydrate; 26.6g protein; 4.5g fibre

notes Recipe is not suitable to freeze. Make and refrigerate the broth the day before so you can chill then remove the fat for a clear broth.

PORK & VEGETABLE WONTON SOUP

prep + cook time 3 hours (+ refrigeration) serves 4

3 litres (12 cups) water
1kg (2 pounds) chicken bones
1 small brown onion (80g), quartered
1 medium carrot (120g), quartered
4cm (1½-inch) piece fresh ginger (20g), grated
2 fresh small red thai (serrano) chillies, halved lengthways
150g (4½ ounces) minced (ground) pork
1 clove garlic, crushed
1 green onion (scallion), chopped finely
2 tablespoons finely chopped water chestnuts
2 tablespoons finely chopped fresh coriander (cilantro)
1 teaspoon sesame oil
2 tablespoons chinese cooking wine
¼ cup (60ml) light soy sauce
2 teaspoons white (granulated) sugar
12 wonton or gow gee wrappers
1 cup firmly packed watercress sprigs
4 fresh shiitake mushrooms, sliced thinly

1 Place the water, chicken bones, brown onion, carrot, three-quarters of the ginger and 2 chilli halves in a large saucepan; bring to the boil. Reduce heat; simmer, covered, 2 hours.

2 Strain broth through a muslin-lined sieve or fine colander into a large heatproof bowl; discard solids. Allow broth to cool; cover, refrigerate so fat solidifies.

3 Chop remaining chilli finely; combine in a medium bowl with remaining ginger, pork, garlic, green onion, water chestnut, coriander, oil, 2 teaspoons of the chinese cooking wine and 1 teaspoon of the sauce and 1 teaspoon of the sugar.

4 Place 1 level tablespoon of filling in the centre of each wonton wrapper; brush edges with a little water. Gather edges around filling; pinch together to seal.

5 Skim and discard fat from surface of broth. Return broth to cleaned saucepan with remaining chinese cooking wine, sauce and sugar; bring to the boil. Add wontons, reduce heat; simmer, uncovered, for 5 minutes or until wontons are cooked. Season broth to taste.

6 Divide watercress, mushrooms and wontons among bowls; ladle broth into bowls.

nutritional count per serving 5.3g total fat (1.6g saturated fat); 853kJ (204 cal); 20.5g carbohydrate; 14.6g protein; 2.4g fibre

notes Uncooked wontons can be frozen; cook, straight from the freezer in the broth. Most Asian grocers stock canned or frozen water chestnuts.

SLOW COOKER PEA & HAM SOUP

prep + cook time 8½ hours **serves** 6

2½ cups (500g) green split peas
1 tablespoon olive oil
1 large brown onion (200g), chopped finely
3 cloves garlic, crushed
1 ham hock (1kg)
2 medium carrots (240g), chopped finely
2 stalks celery (300g), trimmed,
   chopped finely
4 sprigs fresh thyme
2 dried bay leaves
2 litres (8 cups) water

1 Rinse peas under cold water until water runs clear; drain.
2 Heat oil in a large frying pan over medium heat; cook onion and garlic, stirring, until onion softens. Place onion mixture into a 4.5-litre (18-cup) slow cooker; stir in peas and remaining ingredients. Cook, covered, on low, for 8 hours.
3 Remove ham from cooker. When cool enough to handle, remove meat from bone; discard skin, fat and bone. Shred meat coarsely; stir into slow cooker, season to taste.

SERVING SUGGESTION Serve topped with greek-style yoghurt, chopped fresh mint leaves and sliced green onions (scallions).

nutritional count per serving 6.4g total fat (1.2g saturated fat); 1517kJ (363 cal); 43g carbohydrate; 27.3g protein; 11g fibre

notes Recipe suitable to freeze for 1 month. Thaw overnight in the fridge. Reheat in a saucepan or microwave until heated through.

BLACK-EYED BEAN
AND HAM SOUP

prep + cook time 3 hours (+ standing) **serves** 6

1 cup (200g) black-eyed beans
1 tablespoon olive oil
1 stalk celery (150g), trimmed,
   chopped coarsely
1 small brown onion (80g),
   chopped coarsely
1 medium carrot (120g), chopped coarsely
1 dried bay leaf
2 cloves garlic
1.2kg (2½-pound) ham hock
1 litre (4 cups) chicken stock
2 litres (8 cups) water
125g (4 ounces) trimmed silver beet
   (swiss chard), shredded finely
2 tablespoons apple cider vinegar

1 Place beans in a medium bowl, cover with cold water, stand overnight; drain. Rinse under cold water; drain.

2 Heat oil in a large saucepan over medium heat; cook celery, onion and carrot, stirring, until vegetables are soft. Add bay leaf, garlic, ham hock, stock and the water; bring to the boil. Reduce heat; simmer, uncovered, 1 hour.

3 Add beans to soup; simmer, uncovered, about 1 hour or until beans are tender.

4 Remove hock from soup. When cool enough to handle, remove meat from hock. Discard bone, skin and fat; shred meat coarsely, return to soup.

5 Add silver beet to soup; cook, stirring, until wilted. Remove from heat; stir in vinegar. Season to taste.

nutritional count per serving 7.2g total fat (1.8g saturated fat); 945kJ (226 cal); 16.1g carbohydrate; 21.2g protein; 6.3g fibre

notes Recipe is suitable to freeze for 1 month. You need approximately 500g (1 pound) of untrimmed silver beet for this recipe.

MINESTRONE WITH HAM

prep + cook time 4 hours (+ refrigeration) serves 6

1 ham hock (1kg)
1 medium brown onion (150g), quartered
1 stalk celery (150g), trimmed,
    chopped coarsely
1 teaspoon black peppercorns
1 bay leaf
4 litres (16 cups) water
1 tablespoon olive oil
1 large carrot (180g), chopped finely
2 stalks celery (200g), extra, trimmed,
    chopped finely
3 cloves garlic, crushed
¼ cup (70g) tomato paste
2 large tomatoes (440g), chopped finely
1 small leek (200g), sliced thinly
1 cup (100g) small pasta shells
420g (13½ ounces) canned white beans,
    rinsed, drained
½ cup each coarsely chopped fresh
    flat-leaf parsley and basil
½ cup (40g) flaked parmesan

1 Preheat oven to 220°C/425°F.
2 Roast ham hock and onion in a medium baking dish for 30 minutes.
3 Place hock and onion in a large saucepan with celery, peppercorns, bay leaf and the water; bring to the boil. Reduce heat; simmer, uncovered, 2 hours.
4 Remove hock from broth. Strain broth through a muslin-lined sieve or colander into a large heatproof bowl; discard solids. Allow broth to cool. Cover; refrigerate until cold.
5 Remove ham from hock; shred coarsely. Discard bone, fat and skin.
6 Meanwhile, heat oil in cleaned saucepan over medium heat; cook carrot and extra celery, stirring, 2 minutes. Add ham, garlic, paste and tomato; cook, stirring, 2 minutes.
7 Discard fat from surface of broth. Pour broth into a large measuring jug; add enough water to make 2 litres (8 cups). Add broth to pan; bring to the boil. Reduce heat; simmer, covered, 20 minutes.
8 Add leek, pasta and beans to pan; bring to the boil. Reduce heat; simmer, uncovered, until pasta is tender. Remove from heat; stir in herbs. Season to taste.
9 Serve soup topped with parmesan.

nutritional count per serving 7.2g total fat (2.4g saturated fat); 865kJ (207 cal); 19.6g carbohydrate; 12.7g protein; 6.1g fibre

notes Recipe is not suitable to freeze. Make and refrigerate the broth the day before so you can chill then remove the fat for a clear broth.

MEXICAN BEAN & SHREDDED PORK SOUP

prep + cook time 3 hours **serves** 6

2 litres (8 cups) water
2 litres (8 cups) chicken stock
1 large carrot (180g), chopped coarsely
1 stalk celery (150g), trimmed,
   chopped coarsely
5 cloves garlic, unpeeled, bruised
6 black peppercorns
3 sprigs fresh oregano
1 dried bay leaf
1kg (2-pound) piece pork neck
1 tablespoon olive oil
1 large red onion (300g), chopped coarsely
1 medium red capsicum (bell pepper)
   (200g), chopped coarsely
1 medium yellow capsicum (bell pepper)
   (200g), chopped coarsely
2 fresh long red chillies, sliced thinly
2 cloves garlic, crushed
810g (1½ pounds) canned crushed tomatoes
1 teaspoon ground cumin
2 tablespoons coarsely chopped
   fresh oregano
420g (12½ ounces) canned kidney beans,
   rinsed, drained

1 Place the water and stock in a large saucepan with carrot, celery, bruised garlic, peppercorns, oregano sprigs, bay leaf and pork; bring to the boil. Reduce heat; simmer, covered, 1 hour. Uncover; simmer 1 hour.

2 Transfer pork to a medium bowl; using two forks, shred pork coarsely. Strain broth through a muslin-lined sieve or colander into a large heatproof bowl; discard solids.

3 Heat oil in cleaned pan over medium heat; cook onion, capsicum, chilli and crushed garlic, stirring, until vegetables soften. Return pork and broth to pan with undrained tomatoes, cumin and the chopped oregano; bring to the boil. Reduce heat; simmer, covered, 15 minutes. Stir in beans; simmer, covered, until soup is hot. Season to taste.

nutritional count per serving 7.4g total fat (1.6g saturated fat); 1490kJ (356 cal); 20.8g carbohydrate; 46.5g protein; 9.1g fibre

notes Recipe is suitable to freeze. Pork neck may also be sold as pork scotch or foreloin; it is a flavoursome boneless cut.

SLOW COOKER HAM & GREEN LENTIL SOUP

prep + cook time 8½ hours **serves** 6

1.8kg (3½ pounds) meaty ham hocks
½ cup (100g) french-style green lentils
1 tablespoon vegetable oil
2 medium brown onions (300g),
    chopped finely
2 medium carrots (240g), chopped finely
2 stalks celery (300g), trimmed,
    chopped finely
1 teaspoon fresh thyme leaves
2 cups (500ml) salt-reduced chicken stock
1.5 litres (6 cups) water

GREMOLATA
2 cloves garlic, crushed
¼ cup finely chopped fresh flat-leaf parsley
2 teaspoons finely grated lemon rind

1 Rinse ham hocks. Place in a 4.5-litre (18-cup) slow cooker.
2 Rinse lentils under cold water until water runs clear; drain well.
3 Heat oil in a medium frying pan over medium heat; cook onion, stirring, 5 minutes or until softened. Transfer onion to the cooker with carrot, celery, thyme, lentils, stock and the water.
4 Cook, covered, on low, for 8 hours. Carefully remove hock from cooker. When cool enough to handle, remove meat from hock; discard bone, fat and skin. Shred meat finely using two forks. Return meat to cooker. Season to taste.
5 When almost ready to serve, make gremolata; sprinkle over soup to serve. Accompany soup with fresh crusty bread, if you like.

GREMOLATA Combine ingredients in a small bowl.

nutritional count per serving 10.3g total fat (2.8g saturated fat); 1108kJ (265 cal); 12g carbohydrate; 28.6g protein; 5.4g fibre

notes Recipe is not suitable to freeze. Make sure the ham hocks will fit into your slow cooker. Ask the butcher to cut them if they're too large.

BACON, VEGETABLE & RED LENTIL SOUP

prep + cook time 30 minutes **serves** 4

1 tablespoon olive oil

400g (12½-ounce) packet diced fresh
vegetable soup mix (see notes)

2 cloves garlic, crushed

3 rindless bacon slices (195g),
chopped finely

1 cup (200g) red lentils

1 litre (4 cups) salt-reduced chicken stock

2 tablespoons each coarsely chopped fresh
chives and flat-leaf parsley

1 tablespoon finely chopped fresh tarragon

1 Heat oil in a large saucepan over high heat; add soup mix, garlic and bacon. Cook, stirring, until vegetables soften. Add lentils and stock; bring to the boil. reduce heat; simmer, stirring occasionally, for 15 minutes or until lentils are tender and soup has thickened. Season to taste.

2 Serve soup sprinkled with herbs. Accompany with fresh crusty bread rolls, if you like.

nutritional count per serving 13.4g total fat
(3.6g saturated fat); 1417kJ (338 cal);
26g carbohydrate; 24.9g protein; 10.2g fibre

notes Recipe is not suitable to freeze.
Diced fresh vegetable mix can be found in the
chilled vegetable section of major supermarkets.

PORK & UDON SOUP

prep + cook time 25 minutes **serves** 4

1 litre (4 cups) chicken stock
2 cups (500ml) water
1 fresh small red thai (serrano) chilli,
   sliced thinly
10cm (4-inch) stick lemon grass (20g),
   halved lengthways, bruised
2 tablespoons japanese soy sauce
1 teaspoon sesame oil
200g (6½ ounces) fresh udon noodles
100g (3 ounces) fresh shiitake mushrooms,
   sliced thickly
230g (7 ounces) canned bamboo shoots,
   rinsed, drained
40g (1½ ounces) baby spinach leaves
250g (8 ounces) chinese barbecued pork,
   sliced thinly

1 Combine stock, the water, chilli and lemon grass in a large saucepan; bring to the boil. Reduce heat; simmer, covered, 5 minutes. Discard lemon grass.
2 Add sauce, oil, noodles, mushrooms and bamboo shoots to pan; simmer, uncovered, 5 minutes. Season to taste.
3 Divide spinach, pork and noodles into bowls; ladle hot soup over the top.

nutritional count per serving 20.5g total fat (8.9g saturated fat); 1735kJ (415 cal); 31.6g carbohydrate; 22.8g protein; 7.3g fibre

notes Recipe is not suitable to freeze. Chinese barbecued pork has a sweet, sticky coating. It is available from Asian grocery stores.

213

CHINESE PORK IN ORANGE & TAMARIND BROTH

prep + cook time 45 minutes (+ standing) **serves** 8

20g (½ ounce) dried shiitake mushrooms
2 teaspoons vegetable oil
4 shallots (100g), chopped finely
1 clove garlic, crushed
2 fresh small red thai (serrano) chillies, chopped finely
2 litres (8 cups) water
1 litre (4 cups) beef stock
2 teaspoons finely grated orange rind
¼ cup (60ml) orange juice
1 tablespoon tamarind concentrate
400g (14 ounces) chinese barbecued pork, sliced thinly
100g (3 ounces) swiss brown mushrooms, sliced thinly
4 green onions (scallions), sliced thinly

1 Place dried mushrooms in a small bowl, cover with cold water; stand 1 hour. Drain; discard stems, slice caps thinly.

2 Meanwhile, heat oil in a large saucepan over medium heat; cook shallot, garlic and chilli, stirring, 5 minutes or until shallot softens. Add the water, stock, rind, juice and tamarind; bring to the boil.

3 Add pork, shiitake and swiss brown mushrooms to pan. Reduce heat; simmer, covered, 10 minutes or until soup is hot. Season to taste.

4 Serve soup sprinkled with onion.

nutritional count per serving 9.1g total fat (3.4g saturated fat); 648kJ (155 cal); 4.3g carbohydrate; 13.1g protein; 2.1g fibre

notes Recipe is not suitable to freeze. Chinese barbecued pork has a sweet, sticky coating. It is available from Asian grocery stores.

ZUCCHINI, CREAMED CORN & BACON SOUP

prep + cook time 40 minutes **serves** 6

1 tablespoon olive oil

40g (1½ ounces) butter

1 medium brown onion (150g),
   chopped coarsely

4 rindless bacon slices (260g),
   chopped coarsely

4 medium zucchini (480g),
   chopped coarsely

800g (1½ pounds) canned creamed corn

300g (9½ ounces) canned corn kernels,
   rinsed, drained

1 litre (4 cups) chicken stock

2 cups (500ml) water

¾ cup (180ml) evaporated milk

1 Heat oil and butter in a medium saucepan over medium heat; cook onion and bacon, stirring, until onion softens. Add zucchini, creamed corn, corn, stock and the water to pan; cook, covered, stirring occasionally, about 20 minutes.

2 Remove from heat; cool 5 minutes. Stir in evaporated milk; season to taste. Accompany soup with slices of warmed garlic bread, or fresh crusty bread rolls.

nutritional count per serving 17.1g total fat (7.7g saturated fat); 1615kJ (386 cal); 36.5g carbohydrate; 18.2g protein; 7.2g fibre

notes Recipe is not suitable to freeze. Evaporated milk is canned unsweetened milk from which some of the water has been evaporated.

SLOW COOKER CUBAN BLACK BEAN SOUP

prep + cook time 9 hours (+ standing) **serves** 6

1½ cups (300g) dried black beans
1 ham hock (1kg)
2 tablespoons olive oil
1 large brown onion (200g), chopped finely
1 medium red capsicum (bell pepper)
   (200g), chopped finely
3 cloves garlic, crushed
3 teaspoons ground cumin
1 teaspoon dried chilli flakes
400g (12½ ounces) canned crushed tomatoes
2 litres (8 cups) water
3 teaspoons dried oregano leaves
1 teaspoon ground black pepper
2 tablespoons lime juice
1 large tomato (220g), chopped finely
¼ cup coarsely chopped fresh coriander
   (cilantro)

1 Place beans in a medium bowl, cover with cold water, stand overnight; drain. Rinse under cold water; drain.
2 Place beans in a medium saucepan, cover with cold water; bring to the boil. Boil, uncovered, 15 minutes; drain.
3 Meanwhile, preheat oven to 220°C/425°F.
4 Roast ham on oven tray for 30 minutes.
5 Heat oil in a large frying pan over medium heat; cook onion, capsicum and garlic, stirring, until onion is soft. Add cumin and chilli; cook, stirring, until fragrant.
6 Combine beans, ham, onion mixture, canned tomatoes, the water, oregano and pepper in a 4.5-litre (18-cup) slow cooker. Cook, covered, on low, for 8 hours.
7 Remove ham from cooker. When cool enough to handle, remove meat from bone; shred coarsely. Discard skin, fat and bone.
8 Cool soup 10 minutes, then blend or process soup mixture until smooth. Return meat to cooker with pureed soup, stir in juice and chopped tomato. Season to taste. Serve soup sprinkled with coriander.

nutritional count per serving 18.1g total fat (2.9g saturated fat); 1350kJ (323 cal); 9.6g carbohydrate; 24.7g protein; 12.4g fibre

notes Recipe suitable to freeze for 1 month. Thaw overnight in the fridge. Reheat in a saucepan or microwave until heated through.

ROCKET AND PANCETTA SOUP

prep + cook time 1 hour **serves 6**

Make this soup just before serving.

100g (3 ounces) pancetta, sliced thinly
1 tablespoon olive oil
1 medium red onion (170g), chopped coarsely
2 cloves garlic, quartered
1½ tablespoons balsamic vinegar
4 medium potatoes (800g), chopped coarsely
3 cups (750ml) chicken stock
3 cups (750ml) water
500g (1 pound) rocket (arugula), trimmed
¼ cup (20g) finely grated parmesan

1 Preheat oven to 180°C/350°F.
2 Place pancetta in a single layer on an oven tray; roast, uncovered, for 15 minutes or until crisp. Drain pancetta on absorbent paper then chop coarsely.
3 Heat oil in a large saucepan; cook onion and garlic, stirring, until onion softens. Add vinegar and potato; cook, stirring, 5 minutes.
4 Add stock and the water; bring to the boil. Simmer, uncovered, for 15 minutes or until potato softens. Stir in rocket; cook, stirring, about 2 minutes or until rocket is wilted.
5 Blend or process soup mixture, in batches, until smooth. Return soup to pan, stir over heat until hot. Sprinkle soup with cheese and pancetta to serve.

nutritional count per serving 6.9g total fat (2.2g saturated fat); 747kJ (178 cal); 17.9g carbohydrate; 9.4g protein; 2.8g fibre

notes Recipe is not suitable to freeze. Prosciutto can be substituted for the pancetta. Accompany with tomato and basil bruschetta.

PORK TIPS

THE MEAT ON HAM HOCKS IS FULL OF FLAVOUR, BUT NEEDS LONG, SLOW COOKING TO BRING IT OUT. HAM HOCKS MAY ALSO BE SOLD AS 'PORK KNUCKLE'. THE HAM TENDS TO BECOME QUITE SALTY

WHEN FROZEN, SO DON'T FREEZE FOR AS LONG AS OTHER TYPES OF MEAT: UP TO 1 MONTH IS FINE.

IF FREEZING, REMOVE AS MUCH AIR FROM THE CONTAINER AS POSSIBLE TO STOP FREEZER BURN.

MINTED BROAD BEAN & HAM SOUP

prep + cook time 2½ hours **serves** 4

2 teaspoons olive oil

1 large brown onion (200g), chopped coarsely

2 stalks celery (300g), trimmed, chopped coarsely

1 medium carrot (120g), chopped coarsely

2 cloves garlic, crushed

1kg (2-pound) ham hock

2 litres (8 cups) water

3 cups (450g) frozen broad (fava) beans

1 tablespoon lemon juice

⅓ cup finely chopped fresh mint

1 Heat oil in a large saucepan over medium heat; cook onion, celery, carrot and garlic, stirring, until vegetables soften. Add ham hock and the water; bring to the boil. Reduce heat; simmer, covered, for 1½ hours. Uncover; simmer for 30 minutes.

2 Meanwhile, place beans in a medium heatproof bowl, cover with boiling water, stand for 5 minutes; drain. Peel away outer grey skins.

3 Remove ham hock from soup; when cool enough to handle, remove meat from bone, shred coarsely. Discard skin, fat and bone.

4 Add beans to soup; simmer, uncovered, for 5 minutes or until beans are tender. Cool soup for 10 minutes.

5 Using a hand-held blender, blend soup, in pan, until soup is almost smooth. Return ham meat to soup with juice; cook, stirring, until hot. Season to taste.

6 Serve soup topped with mint.

nutritional count per serving 7.4g total fat (2g saturated fat); 890kJ (213 cal); 13.4g carbohydrate; 17.7g protein; 11.4g fibre

notes Recipe suitable to freeze for 1 month. Thaw overnight in the fridge. Reheat in a saucepan or microwave until heated through.

TUSCAN BEAN SOUP

prep + cook time 2¾ hours **serves** 6

2 tablespoons olive oil

3 medium brown onions (450g),
  chopped coarsely

2 cloves garlic, crushed

200g (6½-ounce) piece speck, bacon or
  pancetta, chopped coarsely

2 medium carrots (240g), chopped coarsely

2 stalks celery (300g), trimmed,
  chopped coarsely

800g (1½ pounds) canned crushed tomatoes

¼ medium cabbage (375g),
  shredded coarsely

1 medium zucchini (120g), chopped coarsely

2 sprigs fresh thyme

2 cups (500ml) beef stock

2 litres (8 cups) water

400g (12½ ounces) canned borlotti beans,
  rinsed, drained

6 thick slices ciabatta (250g)

1 Heat oil in a large saucepan over medium heat; cook onion, garlic and speck, stirring, about 5 minutes or until onion is soft.

2 Add carrot, celery, tomatoes, cabbage, zucchini, thyme, stock and the water; bring to the boil. Reduce heat; simmer, uncovered, 2 hours.

3 Add beans; simmer, uncovered, 20 minutes or until beans are tender. Season to taste.

4 Meanwhile, toast bread. Place a slice of bread in the base of each serving bowl, top with soup. Drizzle with extra olive oil before serving, if you like.

nutritional count per serving 12.1g total fat (2.9g saturated fat); 1154kJ (276 cal); 22.8g carbohydrate; 15.2g protein; 8.3g fibre

notes Recipe is not suitable to freeze. Speck is cured, smoked boned hind pork leg; its smoky flavour is great in slow-cooked dishes.

PORK WONTON SOUP

prep + cook time 1¼ hours serves 6

2 teaspoons peanut oil
2 cloves garlic, crushed
2 litres (8 cups) chicken stock
1 tablespoon japanese soy sauce
1 litre (4 cups) water
4 green onions (scallions), sliced thinly

PORK WONTONS
1 tablespoon peanut oil
4 green onions (scallions), sliced thinly
2 cloves garlic, crushed
5cm (2-inch) piece fresh ginger (25g), grated
400g (12½ ounces) minced (ground) pork
2 tablespoons japanese soy sauce
36 wonton wrappers
1 egg, beaten lightly

1 Make pork wontons.

2 Heat oil in a large saucepan over low heat; cook garlic, stirring, 2 minutes. Stir in stock, sauce and the water; bring to the boil. Reduce heat; simmer, uncovered, 15 minutes. Season to taste.

3 Just before serving, divide wontons among serving bowls. Pour over hot soup; sprinkle with onion.

PORK WONTONS Heat oil in a large frying pan over medium heat; cook onion, garlic and ginger, stirring, until onion is soft. Add pork; cook, stirring, until mince is just browned. Stir in sauce; season to taste. Place rounded teaspoons of cooled pork mixture in centre of each wrapper. Brush edges with egg; pinch edges together to seal.

nutritional count per serving 12.3g total fat (3.7g saturated fat); 1225kJ (293 cal); 22.4g carbohydrate; 22.5g protein; 1.6g fibre

notes Freeze broth and wontons separately. Thaw broth overnight in the fridge and reheat until hot; reheat wontons in boiling broth from frozen.

BACON & POTATO SOUP

prep + cook time 45 minutes **serves** 6

6 rindless bacon slices (390g),
  chopped coarsely
4 cloves garlic, crushed
1kg (2 pounds) potatoes, chopped coarsely
2 cups (500ml) water
1 cup (250ml) chicken stock
1¼ cups (300g) sour cream
¼ cup finely chopped fresh flat-leaf parsley

1 Cook bacon and garlic in a heated oiled large saucepan over medium heat, stirring, until bacon is crisp. Add potato, the water and stock; bring to the boil. Reduce heat; simmer, covered, 10 minutes or until potato is tender.

2 Add sour cream; stir until just heated through. Stir in the parsley. Season to taste. Serve soup topped with extra flat-leaf parsley leaves.

nutritional count per serving 26.4g total fat (15.5g saturated fat); 1747kJ (418 cal); 24.1g carbohydrate; 20g protein; 3g fibre

notes Recipe is not suitable to freeze. Warmed or toasted garlic bread is a delicious accompaniment to this soup.

ASIAN BROTH WITH CRISP PORK BELLY

prep + cook time 2½ hours (+ standing & refrigeration) **serves** 4

½ cup (100g) dried soya beans
1½ teaspoons cooking salt (kosher salt)
1 teaspoon chinese five-spice powder
1kg (2-pound) piece boneless pork belly,
   rind scored into diamond shape
2 cups (500ml) water
1 litre (4 cups) chicken stock
1 fresh small red thai (serrano) chilli,
   chopped finely
2 star anise
5cm (2-inch) piece fresh ginger (25g),
   sliced onto fine slivers
⅓ cup (80ml) hoisin sauce
500g (1 pound) choy sum, sliced thinly
3 green onions (scallions), sliced thinly

1 Place beans in a small bowl, cover with cold water, stand overnight; drain. Rinse under cold water; drain.

2 Rub combined salt and half the five-spice into cuts in the pork rind; cut pork into 10 pieces. Place pork, rind-side up, on tray, cover loosely; refrigerate overnight.

3 Preheat oven to 240°C/475°F.

4 Place beans in a medium saucepan of boiling water; return to the boil. Reduce heat; simmer, uncovered, until tender. Drain.

5 Meanwhile, place pork on a metal rack set over a shallow baking dish; roast, uncovered, 30 minutes.

6 Reduce oven to 160°C/325°F; roast pork, uncovered, for a further 45 minutes or until crackling is browned and crisp. Cut pork pieces in half.

7 Place beans in a large saucepan with the water, stock, chilli, star anise, ginger, sauce and remaining five-spice; bring to the boil. Reduce heat; simmer, covered, 30 minutes. Stir in choy sum and onion. Season to taste.

8 Serve soup topped with pork pieces.

nutritional count per serving 59.6g total fat (20.2g saturated fat); 3687kJ (882 cal); 12.4g carbohydrate; 72.2g protein; 6.2g fibre

notes Recipe is not suitable to freeze. Choy sum is available from most greengrocers; all of it is eaten – stems, leaves and flowers.

BACON & LENTIL SOUP

prep + cook time 1 hour **serves** 4

1 tablespoon olive oil

3 rindless bacon slices (195g), chopped coarsely

1 medium brown onion (150g), chopped finely

1 medium carrot (120g), chopped finely

1 stalk celery (150g), trimmed, chopped finely

1 cup (200g) dried brown lentils

410g (12½ ounces) canned crushed tomatoes

1 litre (4 cups) chicken stock

1 dried bay leaf

¼ cup coarsely chopped fresh flat-leaf parsley

1 Heat oil in a large saucepan over medium heat; cook bacon, onion, carrot and celery, stirring, until onion softens.

2 Add lentils, undrained tomatoes, stock and bay leaf; bring to the boil. Reduce heat; simmer, covered, 30 minutes.

3 Discard bay leaf; season to taste. Serve soup sprinkled with parsley.

nutritional count per serving 13.4g total fat (3.7g saturated fat); 1484kJ (355 cal); 27.8g carbohydrate; 26.1g protein; 10.1g fibre

notes Recipe is not suitable to freeze. Use rinsed, drained canned lentils instead of dried; reduce the cooking time in step 2 to 10 minutes.

CHINESE PORK & NOODLE SOUP

prep + cook time 30 minutes **serves** 4

1.5 litres (6 cups) chicken stock
2 cups (500ml) water
8 slices dried shiitake mushrooms
4cm (1½-inch) piece fresh ginger (20g),
  cut into matchsticks
270g (8½ ounces) dried ramen noodles
500g (1 pound) baby pak choy, leaves
  separated
¼ cup (60ml) light soy sauce
⅓ cup (80ml) mirin
400g (12½ ounces) chinese barbecued pork,
  sliced thinly
4 green onions (scallions), sliced thinly
1 fresh long red chilli, sliced thinly
⅓ cup coarsely chopped fresh coriander
  (cilantro)

1 Place stock, the water, mushrooms and ginger in a large saucepan; bring to the boil. Reduce heat; simmer, uncovered, 10 minutes.
2 Meanwhile, cook noodles in a large saucepan of boiling water until tender; drain.
3 Return stock mixture to the boil; add pak choy, simmer until wilted. Stir in sauce and mirin. Season to taste.
4 Divide noodles among serving bowls; top with pork, onion, chilli and coriander. Pour over hot stock mixture.

nutritional count per serving 17g total fat (6.3g saturated fat); 2651kJ (633 cal); 68g carbohydrate; 41.9g protein; 12.7g fibre

notes Recipe is not suitable to freeze. Mirin is sweet rice wine used in Japanese cooking; it is not sake. Available from Asian grocery stores.

PEA, BACON & MINT SOUP

prep + cook time 40 minutes **serves** 4

1 tablespoon olive oil

250g (8 ounces) rindless bacon slices, chopped coarsely

1 medium leek (350g), sliced thinly

1 stalk celery (150g), trimmed, sliced thinly

2 cloves garlic, crushed

880g (1¾ pounds) canned peas, rinsed, drained

1 litre (4 cups) chicken stock

2 cups (500ml) water

1 cup firmly packed fresh mint leaves

1 Heat oil in a large saucepan over medium heat; cook bacon, leek, celery and garlic, stirring, until onion softens and bacon is browned lightly.

2 Add peas, stock, the water and mint to pan; bring to the boil. Reduce heat; simmer, uncovered, 20 minutes. Cool 10 minutes.

3 Blend or process soup, in batches, until almost smooth. Season to taste. Serve with a sprig of mint and a drizzle of oil, if you like.

nutritional count per serving 24.3g total fat (7.8g saturated fat); 1625kJ (388 cal); 17.3g carbohydrate; 20.2g protein; 13.2g fibre

notes Recipe is suitable to freeze.
Wash the leek thoroughly under cold running water to remove any grit between the layers.

ZUPPA DI RISONI

prep + cook time 2¼ hours **serves** 6

This is an Italian pasta and vegetable soup.

4 litres (16 cups) water
3 large carrots (540g), chopped coarsely
2 large brown onions (400g),
   chopped coarsely
4 stalks celery (600g), trimmed,
   chopped coarsely
1 tablespoon black peppercorns
4 dried bay leaves
10 sprigs fresh flat-leaf parsley
1 tablespoon olive oil
1 large brown onion (200g), extra,
   chopped coarsely
2 cloves garlic, crushed
150g (4½-ounce) piece pancetta,
   chopped coarsely
2 medium potatoes (400g), chopped coarsely
2 medium carrots (240g), extra,
   chopped coarsely
2 sprigs fresh rosemary
1 cup (220g) risoni pasta
¼ cup coarsely chopped fresh flat-leaf parsley

1 Combine the water, carrot, onion, celery, peppercorns, bay leaves and parsley sprigs in a large saucepan; bring to the boil. Reduce heat; simmer, uncovered, 1½ hours. Strain stock through a muslin-lined sieve or colander into a large bowl. Discard solids. (The recipe can be made ahead to this stage. Cover; refrigerate overnight or freeze.)
2 Heat oil in a large saucepan over medium heat; cook extra onion, garlic and pancetta, stirring, until onion is soft. Add potato, extra carrot and rosemary sprigs; cook, stirring, for 5 minutes. Stir in stock; bring to the boil. Reduce heat; simmer, uncovered, 10 minutes or until vegetables are tender.
3 Stir in pasta; bring to the boil. Reduce heat; simmer, uncovered, about 5 minutes or until pasta is tender. Season to taste; stir in chopped parsley.

nutritional count per serving 9.6g total fat (2.7g saturated fat); 1418kJ (339 cal); 43.7g carbohydrate; 17.5g protein; 3.8g fibre

notes Recipe is not suitable to freeze. Risoni, a small rice-shaped pasta, can be substituted with orzo or pastina, if you prefer.

CHICKPEA & CHORIZO SOUP

prep + cook time 2 hours (+ refrigeration) **serves** 6

Start this soup the day before serving.

1 tablespoon olive oil
1 large brown onion (200g), chopped finely
2 cloves garlic, crushed
1 cured chorizo sausage (130g), sliced thinly
3 litres (12 cups) water
500g (1-pound) ham bone
4 dried bay leaves
12 sprigs fresh flat-leaf parsley
1 litre (4 cups) water, extra
2 large potatoes (600g), chopped coarsely
600g (1¼ pounds) canned chickpeas
   (garbanzo beans), rinsed, drained
1 cup finely shredded spinach leaves

1 Heat oil in a large saucepan over medium heat; cook onion and garlic, stirring, until onion is soft. Add sausage; cook, stirring, until sausage is browned. Stir in the water, ham bone, bay leaves and parsley; bring to the boil.

2 Reduce heat; simmer, covered, 1½ hours; cool slightly then refrigerate soup mixture, covered, overnight. [Can also be covered and frozen at this stage.]

3 Discard fat from surface of soup mixture. Remove meat from bone; discard bone, skin and fat, shred meat finely.

4 Combine soup mixture with the extra water in a large saucepan; bring to the boil. Stir in ham meat and potato; simmer, covered, about 15 minutes or until potato is tender.

5 Add chickpeas to soup; simmer, uncovered, 5 minutes. Season to taste. Just before serving soup, stir in spinach.

nutritional count per serving 10.1g total fat (2.5g saturated fat); 1131kJ (270 cal); 23.9g carbohydrate; 17.6g protein; 6.7g fibre

notes Recipe is not suitable to freeze. This soup must be assembled, cooked and refrigerated overnight for the flavour to develop.

WHITE BEAN & CHORIZO SOUP

prep + cook time 1¼ hours (+ standing) **serves** 4

1½ cups (300g) dried white beans
1.5 litres (6 cups) water
¼ cup (60ml) olive oil
4 cloves garlic, crushed
⅓ cup coarsely chopped fresh flat-leaf parsley
1 cured chorizo sausage (170g), halved
   lengthways, sliced thinly

1 Place beans in a medium bowl, cover with cold water; stand overnight. Rinse under cold water; drain.

2 Place beans and the water in a large saucepan; simmer, covered, 50 minutes or until tender. Reserve 3 cups cooking liquid; drain beans. Stand 10 minutes. Blend beans and reserved cooking liquid, in batches, until smooth.

3 Heat 2 tablespoons of the oil in cleaned saucepan; stir in garlic, half the parsley and pureed white beans. Simmer, uncovered, 5 minutes. Season to taste.

4 Meanwhile, heat remaining oil in a large frying pan; cook chorizo until browned and crisp.

5 Top soup with chorizo and remaining parsley to serve; drizzle with a little chorizo cooking oil. Accompany with toasted bread or fresh crusty bread rolls, if you like.

nutritional count per serving 36.2g total fat (6.8g saturated fat); 2127kJ (508 cal); 10.7g carbohydrate; 31.1g protein; 16.7g fibre

notes Recipe is suitable to freeze. You can use dried cannellini, haricot, navy or butter beans for this recipe.

245

PASTA, BACON & VEGETABLE SOUP

prep + cook time 1½ hours **serves** 6

2 tablespoons olive oil

1 small brown onion (80g), chopped finely

6 rindless bacon slices (390g),
   chopped coarsely

2.5 litres (10 cups) water

1kg (2 pounds) bacon bones

2 tablespoons tomato paste

3 medium potatoes (600g), quartered

300g (9½ ounces) pumpkin,
   chopped coarsely

200g (6½ ounces) cauliflower,
   chopped coarsely

2½ cups (200g) finely shredded cabbage

1 medium carrot (120g), chopped coarsely

1 cup (110g) frozen beans

1 large zucchini (150g), chopped coarsely

¾ cup (95g) small pasta shells

1 Heat oil in a large saucepan over medium heat; cook onion and bacon slices, stirring, until onion softens.

2 Add the water, bacon bones, paste, potato, pumpkin and cauliflower; bring to the boil. Reduce heat; simmer, covered, for 50 minutes.

3 Remove and discard bacon bones. Using potato masher, roughly crush vegetables.

4 Add cabbage, carrot, beans, zucchini and pasta; simmer, uncovered, for 10 minutes or until pasta is tender. Season to taste.

---

nutritional count per serving 18.5g total fat (5.3g saturated fat); 1760kJ (421 cal); 32.6g carbohydrate; 27.5g protein; 6.8g fibre

notes Recipe is not suitable to freeze. Accompany the soup with fresh or toasted sourdough bread, if you like.

SPEEDY MINESTRONE

prep + cook time 50 minutes **serves** 6

30g (1 ounce) butter

1 medium brown onion (150g), sliced thinly

1 clove garlic, crushed

2 rindless bacon slices (130g),
  chopped coarsely

1 stalk celery (150g), trimmed,
  chopped coarsely

1 medium carrot (120g), chopped coarsely

400g (12½ ounces) canned chopped
  tomatoes

400g (12½ ounces) canned kidney beans,
  rinsed, drained

3 cups (750ml) chicken stock

⅓ cup (60g) spiral pasta

¼ cup (20g) flaked parmesan

2 tablespoons finely chopped fresh
  flat-leaf parsley

1 Melt butter in a large saucepan over medium heat; cook onion, garlic and bacon, stirring, until onion softens. Add celery and carrot; cook, stirring, 2 minutes.

2 Stir in tomatoes, beans, stock and pasta; bring to the boil. Reduce heat; simmer, covered, 30 minutes. Season to taste. Serve topped with cheese and parsley.

nutritional count per serving 7.9g total fat (4.3g saturated fat); 752kJ (180 cal); 17.6g carbohydrate; 9.6g protein; 4.6g fibre

notes Recipe is not suitable to freeze. Minestrone can be made up to two days ahead; store, covered, in the refrigerator.

SMOKY HAM AND RED LENTIL SOUP

prep + cook time 35 minutes **serves** 4

1 large brown onion (200g), chopped finely
1 fresh long red chilli, sliced thinly
2 tablespoons mild curry paste
1 litre (4 cups) vegetable stock
1 litre (4 cups) water
800g (1½ pounds) canned diced tomatoes
1 cup (200g) red lentils, rinsed
200g (6½-ounce) piece smoked ham, cut
   into 1cm (½-inch) pieces
300g (4½ ounces) baby spinach leaves
½ cup loosely packed fresh coriander
   leaves (cilantro)

1 Heat medium non-stick saucepan over medium heat; cook onion and chilli, stirring, until onion softens. Add curry paste; cook, stirring, 1 minute or until fragrant.
2 Add stock, the water, undrained tomatoes and lentils; bring to the boil. Reduce heat; simmer, covered, 20 minutes or until lentils are tender. Stir in ham and spinach; return to the boil. Season to taste.
3 Serve soup topped with coriander.

nutritional count per serving 8.4g total fat (1.4g saturated fat); 1408kJ (336 cal); 31.8g carbohydrate; 28.1g protein; 13.4g fibre

notes Recipe is not suitable to freeze.
For those requiring a curry paste with little heat, massaman and korma are both relatively mild.

250

SMOKY CHEDDAR & MUSTARD SCONES

prep + cook time 35 minutes **makes** 12

Preheat oven to 240°C/475°F. Grease a deep 19cm (8-inch) square cake pan. Sift 1 cup self-raising flour into a large bowl; rub in 50g (1½oz) butter. Stir in 1 lightly beaten egg, ½ cup coarsely grated smoked cheddar, 1 tablespoon wholegrain mustard and about ¼ cup (60ml) milk to make a soft, sticky dough. Turn dough onto a floured surface; knead gently until smooth. Press dough out evenly into a 2cm (¾-inch) thickness. Use a 5cm (2-inch) round cutter to cut rounds from dough; place side by side, just touching, in pan. Gently knead dough scraps together; repeat pressing and cutting out scones. Bake scones about 15 minutes.

GOAT'S CHEESE SCONES

prep + cook time 35 minutes **makes** 12

Preheat oven to 240°C/475°F. Grease a deep 19cm (8-inch) square cake pan. Sift 1 cup self-raising flour into a large bowl; rub in 50g (1½oz) butter. Stir in 1 lightly beaten egg, 100g (3oz) crumbled goat's cheese, ¼ cup coarsely grated parmesan, 1 tablespoon finely chopped fresh chives and about ¼ cup (60ml) milk to make a soft, sticky dough. Turn dough onto a floured surface; knead gently until smooth. Press dough out evenly into a 2cm (¾-inch) thickness. Use a 5cm (2-inch) round cutter to cut rounds from dough; place side by side, just touching, in pan. Gently knead dough scraps together; repeat pressing and cutting out scones. Bake scones about 15 minutes.

SUN-DRIED TOMATO SCONES

prep + cook time 35 minutes **makes** 12

Preheat oven to 240°C/475°F. Grease a deep 19cm (8-inch) square cake pan. Sift 1 cup self-raising flour into a large bowl; rub in 50g (1½oz) butter. Stir in 1 lightly beaten egg, ¼ cup coarsely grated parmesan, ¼ cup finely chopped fresh flat-leaf parsley, ⅓ cup finely chopped sun-dried tomatoes and about ¼ cup (60ml) milk to make a soft, sticky dough. Turn dough onto a floured surface; knead gently until smooth. Press dough out evenly into a 2cm (¾-inch) thickness. Use a 5cm (2-inch) round cutter to cut rounds from dough; place side by side, just touching, in pan. Gently knead dough scraps together; repeat pressing and cutting out scones. Bake scones about 15 minutes.

PARSLEY AND CHIVE SCONES

prep + cook time 35 minutes **makes** 12

Preheat oven to 240°C/475°F. Grease a deep 19cm (8-inch) square cake pan. Sift 1 cup self-raising flour into a large bowl; rub in 50g (1½oz) butter. Stir in 1 lightly beaten egg, 2 tablespoons finely chopped fresh flat-leaf parsley, 2 tablespoons finely chopped fresh chives and about ⅓ cup (80ml) milk to make a soft, sticky dough. Turn dough onto floured surface; knead gently until smooth. Press the dough out evenly into a 2cm (¾-inch) thickness. Use a 5cm (2-inch) round cutter to cut rounds from dough; place side by side, just touching, in pan. Gently knead dough scraps together; repeat pressing and cutting out scones. Bake scones about 15 minutes.

253

VEGETABLE

KUMARA SOUP WITH ROSEMARY SOURDOUGH

prep + cook time 40 minutes (+ cooling) **serves** 6

1 tablespoon olive oil

2 medium kumara (orange sweet potatoes) (800g), chopped coarsely

1 medium brown onion (150g), chopped coarsely

2 cloves garlic, quartered

2 teaspoons coarsely chopped fresh rosemary

1 teaspoon finely grated lemon rind

2 cups (500ml) vegetable stock

2 cups (500ml) water

1 tablespoon lemon juice

½ cup (125ml) pouring cream

ROSEMARY SOURDOUGH

2 tablespoons olive oil

2 teaspoons finely chopped fresh rosemary

1 loaf sourdough bread (675g), cut into 3cm (1¼-inch) slices

1 Heat oil in a large saucepan over medium heat; cook kumara, onion and garlic, stirring, 10 minutes. Add rosemary, rind, stock and the water; bring to the boil. Reduce heat; simmer, covered, 15 minutes or until kumara is soft. Cool 15 minutes.

2 Meanwhile, make rosemary sourdough.

3 Blend or process soup, in batches, until smooth. Return soup to pan, add juice; stir over medium heat until hot, season.

4 Serve bowls of soup drizzled with cream; accompany with rosemary sourdough.

ROSEMARY SOURDOUGH Preheat oven to 180°C/350°F. Combine oil and rosemary in a small bowl. Place bread on an oven tray; brush both sides with oil mixture. Bake bread slices, 15 minutes, turning halfway, until toasted and golden.

nutritional count per serving 21g total fat (7.8g saturated fat); 2257kJ (540 cal); 69.1g carbohydrate; 15.7g protein; 5.6g fibre

notes Recipe is suitable to freeze. You can also make the soup up to two days ahead; store, covered, in the refrigerator.

CREAM OF SPINACH SOUP WITH LEMON FETTA TOAST

prep + cook time 55 minutes (+ cooling) serves 6

40g (1½ ounces) butter
1 large brown onion (200g), chopped finely
2 cloves garlic, crushed
3 medium potatoes (600g), chopped coarsely
3 cups (750ml) vegetable stock
1 litre (4 cups) water
250g (8 ounces) trimmed spinach,
   chopped coarsely
¾ cup (180ml) pouring cream
½ cup loosely packed fresh flat-leaf
   parsley leaves

LEMON FETTA TOAST
150g (4½ ounces) fetta cheese
2 teaspoons finely grated lemon rind
1 small french bread stick (150g), cut
   into 2cm (¾-inch) slices

1 Melt butter in a large saucepan over medium heat; cook onion and garlic, stirring, until onion softens. Add potato, stock and the water; bring to the boil. Reduce heat; simmer, covered, about 15 minutes or until potato is tender. Stir in spinach; cool 15 minutes.
2 Meanwhile, make lemon fetta toasts.
3 Blend or process soup, in batches, until smooth. Return soup to pan, add cream; stir over medium heat until hot. Season to taste.
4 Serve bowls of soup sprinkled with parsley; accompany with toast.

LEMON FETTA TOAST Preheat grill (broiler). Combine cheese with 1 teaspoon of the rind in a small bowl. Discard end pieces of bread; place slices on oven tray. Toast slices one side; turn, sprinkle each slice with fetta mixture and remaining rind. Grill toasts until browned lightly.

nutritional count per serving 25.7g total fat (16.2g saturated fat); 1622kJ (388 cal); 26.1g carbohydrate; 11.6g protein; 4g fibre

notes Recipe is not suitable to freeze. You need 1kg (2 pounds) of untrimmed spinach to get the amount of trimmed spinach needed.

GAZPACHO

prep time 25 minutes (+ refrigeration) **serves** 6

1kg (2 pounds) ripe tomatoes, peeled, chopped coarsely

2 lebanese cucumbers (260g), seeded, chopped coarsely

2 large red capsicums (bell peppers) (700g), chopped coarsely

1 large green capsicum (bell pepper) (350g), chopped coarsely

1 large red onion (300g), chopped coarsely

2 cloves garlic, chopped coarsely

415g (13 ounces) canned tomato juice

2 tablespoons red wine vinegar

1 tablespoon olive oil

2 teaspoons Tabasco sauce

1 medium avocado (250g), chopped finely

1 small yellow capsicum (bell pepper) (150g), chopped finely

¼ cup finely chopped fresh coriander (cilantro)

1 Blend or process tomato, cucumber, red and green capsicum, onion, garlic, juice, vinegar, oil and sauce, in batches, until smooth. Pour into large jug. Cover; refrigerate 3 hours.

2 Stir soup, season to taste; pour into serving bowls, top with remaining ingredients. Serve gazpacho sprinkled with extra Tabasco, if you like.

nutritional count per serving 10.4g total fat (1.9g saturated fat); 786kJ (188 cal); 14.5g carbohydrate; 6.2g protein; 6.3g fibre

notes Suitable to freeze at the end of step 1. Gazpacho is usually a chilled tomato-based soup, but other varieties, such as cucumber, do exist.

MINESTRONE

prep + cook time 2 hours (+ standing) **serves** 6

1 cup (200g) dried borlotti beans

1 tablespoon olive oil

1 medium brown onion (150g),
   chopped coarsely

1 clove garlic, crushed

¼ cup (70g) tomato paste

1.5 litres (6 cups) water

2 cups (500ml) vegetable stock

2⅔ cups (700g) bottled tomato pasta sauce
   (passata)

1 stalk celery (150g), trimmed, chopped
   finely

1 medium carrot (120g), chopped finely

1 medium zucchini (120g), chopped finely

80g (2½ ounces) green beans, trimmed,
   chopped finely

¾ cup (135g) macaroni pasta

⅓ cup coarsely chopped fresh basil

1 Place borlotti beans in a medium bowl, cover with water; stand overnight, drain. Rinse under cold water; drain.

2 Heat oil in a large saucepan over medium heat; cook onion and garlic, stirring, until onion softens. Add paste; cook, stirring, 2 minutes. Add borlotti beans to pan with the water, stock and pasta sauce; bring to the boil. Reduce heat; simmer, uncovered, about 1 hour or until beans are tender.

3 Add celery; simmer, uncovered, 10 minutes. Add carrot, zucchini and green beans; simmer, uncovered, about 20 minutes or until carrot is tender. Add pasta; simmer until pasta is tender. Season to taste.

4 Serve soup sprinkled with basil.

nutritional count per serving 5.5g total fat (1g saturated fat); 1095kJ (262 cal); 39.9g carbohydrate; 9.4g protein; 6.5g fibre

notes Recipe is not suitable to freeze. Borlotti beans, also known as roman or pink beans, are interchangeable with pinto beans.

CURRIED CAULIFLOWER SOUP

prep + cook time 25 minutes **serves** 4

¼ cup (75g) red curry paste
½ small cauliflower (500g), chopped coarsely
2 medium potatoes (400g), chopped coarsely
2 litres (8 cups) water
1 tablespoon lime juice

1 Stir paste in a heated large saucepan, over high heat, for 3 minutes or until paste is fragrant.
2 Add cauliflower, potato and the water; bring to the boil. Reduce heat; simmer, uncovered, 15 minutes or until vegetables are tender. Cool 10 minutes.
3 Blend or process soup, in batches, until smooth. Stir in juice; season to taste. Return soup to pan to heat through.

nutritional count per serving 7.6g total fat (0.8g saturated fat); 777kJ (186 cal); 17.3g carbohydrate; 7.9g protein; 7.2g fibre

notes Recipe is suitable to freeze.
Sprinkle the soup with fresh coriander (cilantro) leaves and a pinch of hot paprika.

VEGETABLE DUMPLINGS IN BROTH

prep + cook time 1¼ hours **serves** 4

100g (3 ounces) fresh shiitake mushrooms

2 green onions (scallions)

1 medium brown onion (150g), chopped coarsely

1 medium carrot (120g), chopped coarsely

2 cloves garlic, chopped coarsely

2cm (¾-inch) piece fresh ginger (10g), chopped coarsely

1 star anise

1 teaspoon sichuan peppercorns

¼ cup (60ml) japanese soy sauce

2 tablespoons chinese cooking wine

4 fresh coriander (cilantro) roots

1 teaspoon white (granulated) sugar

1.5 litres (6 cups) water

800g (1½ pounds) buk choy

1cm (½-inch) piece fresh ginger (5g), extra, grated

1 clove garlic, extra, crushed

227g (7 ounces) canned water chestnuts, drained, chopped finely

1 egg white, beaten lightly

¼ cup (15g) stale breadcrumbs

2 tablespoons finely chopped fresh coriander (cilantro)

1 tablespoon vegetarian oyster sauce

20 wonton or gow gee wrappers

100g (3 ounces) enoki mushrooms, trimmed

1 Separate stems from shiitake mushroom caps; reserve stems and caps. Finely chop a quarter of the caps; slice remaining caps thinly. Coarsely chop white section of green onion. Thinly slice green section; reserve.

2 Combine shiitake stems, white section of green onion, brown onion, carrot, garlic, ginger, star anise, peppercorns, soy sauce, wine, coriander roots, sugar and the water in a large saucepan; bring to the boil. Reduce heat; simmer, uncovered, 45 minutes. Strain through a fine sieve into large heatproof bowl; discard solids. Return stock to pan; bring to the boil. Reduce heat; simmer, covered.

3 Separate buk choy bases and leaves. Finely chop half the bases; discard remaining bases. Combine bases with finely chopped shiitake mushrooms, extra ginger, extra garlic, water chestnuts, egg white, breadcrumbs, coriander leaves and oyster sauce in a large bowl.

4 To make dumplings: place a heaped teaspoon of the mushroom mixture in centre of a wonton wrapper; brush edges with a little water. Fold wrapper in half diagonally; pinch edges together to seal. Repeat with remaining mixture and wrappers. Add enoki and sliced shiitake mushrooms to stock; cook 5 minutes. Add dumplings; cook 5 minutes or until cooked through. Stir in buk choy leaves.

5 Top soup with green onion to serve.

nutritional count per serving 1.6g total fat (0.2g saturated fat); 978kJ (234 cal); 40g carbohydrate; 11.6g protein; 6.8g fibre

notes Recipe is not suitable to freeze. Vegetarian oyster sauce can be found in most supermarkets and Asian food stores.

TOFU AND SPINACH MISO

prep + cook time 20 minutes **serves** 4

1.5 litres (6 cups) water
¼ cup (75g) yellow miso
1 tablespoon japanese soy sauce
3cm (1¼-inch) piece fresh ginger (15g), grated
100g (3 ounces) dried soba noodles
200g (6½ ounces) teriyaki-flavoured tofu, cut into 2cm (¾-inch) pieces
4 green onions (scallions), sliced thinly
100g (3 ounces) baby spinach leaves
1 fresh long red chilli, sliced thinly

1 Place the water, yellow miso, sauce and ginger in a large saucepan; bring to the boil. Add noodles, return to the boil; cook, uncovered, about 3 minutes or until noodles are just tender.
2 Remove from heat, add tofu, onion and spinach to broth; stir gently until spinach wilts.
3 Serve bowls of soup sprinkled with chilli.

nutritional count per serving 4.9g total fat (0.7g saturated fat); 803kJ (192 cal); 22.9g carbohydrate; 12.1g protein; 3.8g fibre

notes Recipe is not suitable to freeze. Yellow miso (shinshu), is a smooth, deep-yellow, fairly salty, tart, fermented soya bean paste.

PRESSURE COOKER SPICY CHICKPEA & LENTIL SOUP

prep + cook time 40 minutes (+ standing) **serves** 6

1 cup (200g) dried chickpeas
(garbanzo beans)
2 teaspoons olive oil
1 medium brown onion (150g),
chopped finely
3 cloves garlic, crushed
4cm (1½-inch) piece fresh ginger (20g),
grated coarsely
2 teaspoons smoked paprika
1 teaspoon each ground cumin and coriander
½ teaspoon dried chilli flakes
410g (13 ounces) canned crushed tomatoes
1 litre (4 cups) water
2 cups (500ml) vegetable stock
2 stalks celery (300g), trimmed, sliced thickly
470g (15 ounces) pumpkin, cut into
1cm (½-inch) pieces
1 cup (200g) red lentils, rinsed, drained
2 tablespoons lime juice
½ cup coarsely chopped fresh coriander
(cilantro)

1 Place chickpeas in a medium bowl, cover with cold water; stand overnight, drain. Rinse under cold water; drain.
2 Heat oil in a 6-litre (24-cup) pressure cooker; cook onion, garlic and ginger, stirring, until onion softens. Add spices; cook, stirring, until fragrant. Add tomatoes, the water, stock and chickpeas; secure lid. Bring cooker to high pressure according to manufacturer's instructions. Reduce heat to stabilise pressure; cook 25 minutes.
3 Release the steam pressure according to the manufacturer's instructions; remove lid. Add celery, pumpkin and lentils; secure lid. Bring cooker to high pressure. Reduce heat to stabilise pressure; cook 5 minutes.
4 Release the steam pressure according to manufacturer's instructions; remove lid. Stir in juice and coriander; season to taste.

nutritional count per serving 4g total fat (0.6g saturated fat); 940kJ (224 cal); 28.9g carbohydrate; 13.7g protein; 10.2g fibre

notes Recipe is suitable to freeze. Always check the manufacturer's instructions before using a pressure cooker.

PRESSURE COOKER RICE, CHICKPEA & YOGHURT SOUP

prep + cook time 40 minutes (+ standing) **serves** 6

1 cup (200g) dried chickpeas
   (garbanzo beans)
2 litres (8 cups) water
½ cup (125ml) olive oil
2 large brown onions (400g), sliced thinly
1 cup (200g) jasmine rice
500g (1 pound) greek-style yoghurt
1½ cups loosely packed fresh mint leaves

1 Place chickpeas in a medium bowl, cover with cold water, stand overnight; drain. Rinse under cold water; drain.
2 Combine chickpeas and half the water in a 6-litre (24-cup) pressure cooker; secure lid. Bring cooker to high pressure according to manufacturer's instructions. Reduce heat to stabilise pressure, if required; cook 10 minutes.
3 Meanwhile, heat 2 tablespoons of the oil in a large frying pan over medium heat; cook onion, stirring, about 5 minutes or until browned lightly. Remove half the onion from pan; reserve. Cook remaining onion, stirring, about 8 minutes or until caramelised.

4 Release the steam pressure according to manufacturer's instructions; remove lid. Stir in rice, reserved onion and the remaining water; secure lid.
5 Bring cooker to high pressure. Reduce heat to stabilise pressure, if required; cook 5 minutes. Release pressure according to manufacturer's instructions: remove lid. Stir in yoghurt; simmer, uncovered, until hot. Season to taste.
6 Meanwhile, heat remaining oil in a small saucepan over high heat; deep-fry mint, in batches, until bright green. Remove with a slotted spoon; drain on absorbent paper.
7 Serve soup topped with caramelised onion and fried mint.

nutritional count per serving 26.2g total fat (6.3g saturated fat); 2170kJ (518 cal); 52.8g carbohydrate; 13.4g protein; 6.6g fibre

notes Recipe is not suitable to freeze. Be careful when frying mint as it will spit. Store cooled leaves in an airtight container for 1-2 days.

HOT & SOUR VEGETABLE SOUP

prep + cook time 25 minutes **serves** 4

180g (5½ ounces) dried soba noodles
2 tablespoons tom yum paste
4 fresh kaffir lime leaves, crushed
2 fresh long red chillies, halved
1 litre (4 cups) water
1 litre (4 cups) vegetable stock
2 large carrot (360g), cut into matchsticks
2 medium red capsicum (bell pepper)
   (300g), sliced thinly
200g (6½ ounces) button mushrooms,
   sliced thinly
500g (1 pound) broccolini,
   chopped coarsely
200g (6½ ounces) snow peas, sliced thinly
4 green onions (scallions), sliced thinly
¼ cup (60ml) lime juice
1 tablespoon fish sauce
1 cup (80g) bean sprouts
2 tablespoons fresh mint leaves
2 tablespoons fresh coriander leaves
   (cilantro)

1 Cook noodles in a large saucepan of boiling water until tender; drain.
2 Heat a large non-stick saucepan over medium heat; cook paste, lime leaves and chilli, stirring, until fragrant. Add the water and stock; bring to the boil while stirring.
3 Reduce heat; simmer 5 minutes. Add carrot, capsicum, mushrooms, broccolini and snow peas; simmer, uncovered, 5 minutes or until vegetables are tender.
4 Stir in onion, juice and sauce; season to taste. Discard lime leaves and chilli. Divide noodles between bowls; ladle soup over noodles, top with sprouts and herbs.

nutritional count per serving 5.4g total fat (0.7g saturated fat); 1672kJ (400 cal); 59.4g carbohydrate; 21.3g protein; 13.3g fibre

notes Recipe is not suitable to freeze. Reheat soup in the microwave on HIGH (100%) for 1½ minutes, stirring halfway through.

FENNEL & TOMATO SOUP WITH ROUILLE

prep + cook time 30 minutes **serves** 4

1 medium leek (350g)

1 large fennel bulb (550g)

¼ cup (60ml) extra virgin olive oil

1 medium brown onion (150g),
chopped coarsely

1 stalk celery (150g), trimmed,
chopped coarsely

3 cloves garlic, crushed

pinch saffron threads

800g (1½ pounds) canned diced tomatoes

1 litre (4 cups) vegetable stock

2 medium potatoes (400g), cut into
1.5cm (¾-inch) pieces

8 x 1.5cm (¾-inch) thick slices sourdough
bread (380g)

ROUILLE

⅔ cup (200g) whole-egg mayonnaise

3 teaspoons lemon juice

3 teaspoons tomato paste

2 cloves garlic, crushed

pinch saffron threads

¼ teaspoon cayenne pepper

1 Quarter leek lengthways; slice thinly. Reserve fennel tops; chop fennel finely.

2 Heat half the oil in a large saucepan over medium heat; cook leek, fennel, onion and celery, stirring, 5 minutes or until softened. Add garlic and saffron; cook, stirring, until fragrant. Add tomatoes, stock and potato; bring to the boil. Reduce heat; simmer, covered, 10 minutes or until tender. Season to taste. Cover to keep hot.

3 Meanwhile, make rouille.

4 Heat a grill pan (or grill or barbecue). Brush bread on both sides with remaining oil; cook until browned lightly on both sides.

5 Ladle soup into serving bowls; top with reserved fennel tops. Serve with toasted bread and rouille.

ROUILLE Combine ingredients in a small bowl; season to taste.

---

nutritional count per serving 58.3g total fat (9.4g saturated fat); 3825kJ (914 cal); 74.4g carbohydrate; 17.8g protein; 13g fibre

notes Soup can be frozen at the end of step 2. Rouille (a French sauce meaning 'rust' because of its reddish colour) can be made a day ahead.

276

SPINACH, ROCKET & PEA SOUP WITH BRIE CROÛTES

prep + cook time 35 minutes **serves** 4

40g (1½ ounces) butter
1 medium leek (350g), sliced thinly
1 clove garlic, crushed
1 large potato (300g), chopped coarsely
1 litre (4 cups) vegetable stock
1 cup (250ml) water
1 cup (120g) frozen peas
270g (8½ ounces) spinach, trimmed
30g (1 ounce) baby rocket leaves (arugula)
½ cup (125ml) pouring cream

BRIE CROÛTES
12 slices (120g) sourdough baguette
1 tablespoon dijon mustard
150g (4½ ounces) brie cheese

1 Melt butter in a large saucepan over medium heat; cook leek, stirring, 5 minutes or until soft but not coloured. Add garlic; cook, stirring, until fragrant.
2 Add potato, stock and the water to pan; bring to the boil. Reduce heat; simmer, uncovered, 10 minutes or until potato is tender. Add peas, spinach and rocket; simmer, uncovered, 5 minutes. Remove from heat; stand soup 10 minutes.
3 Blend soup, in batches, until smooth. Return soup to pan; stir in cream until hot over medium heat. Season to taste.
4 Meanwhile, make brie croûtes.
5 Ladle soup into serving bowls; serve with croûtes and freshly ground black pepper.

BRIE CROÛTES Preheat grill (broiler) to high. Place bread under grill until browned lightly on one side. Turn bread, spread with mustard and top with slices of cheese. Grill until melted slightly.

nutritional count per serving 33.2g total fat (20.4g saturated fat); 2088kJ (500 cal); 29.5g carbohydrate; 18g protein; 7.3g fibre

notes Recipe is suitable to freeze.
A blender will produce a smoother, finer textured soup than a food processor.

279

PRIMAVERA SOUP WITH PANGRATTATO

prep + cook time 25 minutes serves 4

30g (1 ounce) butter
4 shallots (100g), chopped finely
1 litre (4 cups) vegetable stock
2 cups (500ml) water
⅓ cup (75g) risoni pasta
250g (8 ounces) baby green zucchini,
   halved lengthways
150g (4½ ounces) asparagus, cut into 3cm
   (1¼-inch) lengths
2 cups (240g) frozen baby peas

PANGRATTATO

200g (6½ ounces) crusty italian-style bread
2 tablespoons extra virgin olive oil
1 fresh long red chilli, sliced thinly
2 cloves garlic, chopped finely
⅓ cup loosely packed small flat-leaf
   parsley leaves
1 teaspoon finely grated lemon rind

1 Melt butter in a large saucepan over medium heat; cook shallots, stirring, 3 minutes or until soft.
2 Add stock and the water to pan; bring to the boil. Add pasta and zucchini; simmer, uncovered, 5 minutes, stirring occasionally.
3 Meanwhile, make pangrattato.
4 Add asparagus and peas to soup; simmer, uncovered, 5 minutes or until just tender. Season to taste.
5 Ladle soup into bowls; top with pangrattato.

PANGRATTATO Remove crust from bread; tear into 1cm (½-inch) pieces. Heat oil in a large frying pan over medium-high heat; cook chilli and bread pieces, stirring, until browned lightly and crisp. Add garlic; cook until fragrant. Remove from heat; stir in parsley and rind. Season to taste.

nutritional count per serving 17.7g total fat (5.9g saturated fat); 1760kJ (420 cal); 46.7g carbohydrate; 14.3g protein; 9.2g fibre

notes Recipe is not suitable to freeze. Make soup just before serving, as it will discolour on standing. Pangrattato is Italian for breadcrumbs.

CHICKPEA AND BROAD BEAN SOUP WITH EGGS

prep + cook time 35 minutes **serves** 6

1 tablespoon extra virgin olive oil

1 medium brown onion (150g), chopped coarsely

2 medium carrots (240g), chopped coarsely

2 stalks celery (300g), trimmed, chopped coarsely

2 cloves garlic, chopped

2 teaspoons each ground cumin, coriander and paprika

½ teaspoon ground cinnamon

400g (12½ ounces) canned diced tomatoes

1.5 litres (6 cups) vegetable stock

½ cup (100g) french-style green lentils, rinsed, drained

400g (12½ ounces) canned chickpeas (garbanzo beans), rinsed, drained

2 cups (320g) frozen broad (fava) beans

¼ cup coarsely chopped fresh flat-leaf parsley

¼ cup coarsely chopped fresh coriander (cilantro)

4 eggs

¼ teaspoon ground cumin, extra

½ teaspoon sea salt flakes

lemon wedges, for serving

1 Heat oil in a large saucepan over medium heat; cook onion, carrot, celery and garlic, stirring, 5 minutes or until softened. Add spices; cook, stirring, until fragrant.

2 Add tomatoes and stock; bring to the boil. Add lentils and chickpeas; simmer, uncovered, 10 minutes.

3 Meanwhile, pour boiling water over broad beans in a heatproof bowl; stand 2 minutes, drain. Peel beans.

4 Add beans to the pan; simmer, uncovered, a further 5 minutes or until lentils are tender. Stir in half the herbs; season to taste.

5 Meanwhile, place eggs in a small saucepan; cover with cold water. Bring to the boil; simmer, uncovered, for 3 minutes. Drain; run under cold water until cool enough to handle. Peel eggs; chop coarsely.

6 Ladle soup into serving bowls; top with egg, remaining herbs and combined extra cumin and salt. Serve with lemon wedges.

SERVING SUGGESTION Warm afghan or turkish bread.

---

nutritional count per serving 9.1g total fat (2g saturated fat); 1103kJ (263 cal); 23.1g carbohydrate; 17.6g protein; 11.7g fibre

notes The soup can be prepared to the end of step 3 up to 6 hours ahead; store, covered, in the fridge. Soup is not suitable to freeze.

283

VEGETABLE TIPS

FOR SOUP BURSTING WITH FLAVOUR, BUY ONLY THE FRESHEST VEGETABLES THAT ARE IN SEASON. VEGETABLES THAT ARE REFRIGERATED LONG TERM IN COLD-STORAGE UNITS WILL LOSE FLAVOUR,

WHICH IS REFLECTED IN BLAND-TASTING SOUP. YOU DON'T ALWAYS NEED TO BLEND SOUP UNTIL IT'S COMPLETELY SMOOTH, LEAVE SOME UNBLENDED FOR ADDED TEXTURE, OR ADD SOME PASTA.

VICHYSSOISE

prep + cook time 45 minutes (+ refrigeration) **serves** 4

This thick, creamy, potato and leek flavoured soup is usually served cold.

30g (1 ounce) butter
1 large brown onion (200g), chopped finely
1 large leek (500g), sliced thickly
4 medium potatoes (800g), chopped coarsely
1.5 litres (6 cups) vegetable stock
300ml pouring cream
2 tablespoons finely chopped fresh chives

1 Melt butter in a large saucepan over medium heat; cook onion and leek, stirring, for 10 minutes or until soft. Add potato and stock; bring to the boil. Reduce heat; simmer, covered, for 15 minutes.
2 Stand 10 minutes, then blend or process soup, in batches, until smooth. Stir in cream; cover, refrigerate 3 hours or overnight.
3 Season soup to taste; serve sprinkled with chives.

nutritional count per serving 40.6g total fat (26.3g saturated fat); 2299kJ (550 cal); 32.8g carbohydrate; 12g protein; 5.6g fibre

notes Recipe is not suitable to freeze. Before using, leeks should to be washed to remove any grit from the inside layers.

CORN SOUP WITH PARMESAN CRISPS & CHILLI

prep + cook time 40 minutes (+ cooling) **serves** 4

8 trimmed corn cobs (2kg)
30g (1 ounce) butter
1 large brown onion (200g), chopped finely
2 cups (500ml) vegetable stock
1 cup (250ml) water
1 cup (250ml) thickened (heavy) cream
1 tablespoon vegetable oil
1 fresh long red chilli, sliced thinly
⅔ cup (10g) puffed corn
2 tablespoons fresh baby coriander leaves
   (cilantro)

PARMESAN CRISPS
⅓ cup (25g) finely grated parmesan

1 Cut kernels from corn cobs.
2 Melt butter in a large saucepan over medium heat; cook onion, stirring, until soft but not coloured. Add stock and the water; bring to the boil. Add corn kernels; simmer, covered, 20 minutes or until corn is tender. Stand 10 minutes.
3 Meanwhile, make parmesan crisps.
4 Blend half the soup mixture until smooth; return to the pan. Stir in cream over medium heat until hot. Season to taste.
5 Heat oil in a small frying pan over medium heat; cook chilli, stirring, until soft.
6 Ladle soup into serving bowls; top with puffed corn, chilli and the oil, then coriander. Serve with parmesan crisps.

PARMESAN CRISPS Preheat oven to 180°C/350°F. Line a large oven tray with baking paper. Sprinkle parmesan in a thin layer on tray; flatten slightly. Bake 8 minutes or until browned lightly. Cool on tray. Break into pieces when cold.

nutritional count per serving 40.1g total fat (20.7g saturated fat); 2503kJ (598 cal); 37.6g carbohydrate; 15.2g protein; 15.1g fibre

notes Recipe is not suitable to freeze. Puffed corn is whole grain corn steamed until it puffs up. It's available from health food stores.

ROASTED CAPSICUM SOUP WITH POLENTA FINGERS

prep + cook time 1¾ hours (+ refrigeration) **serves** 6

4 medium red capsicums (bell peppers)
(800g)
2 cloves garlic, unpeeled
1 tablespoon olive oil
1 medium brown onion (150g),
chopped finely
1 teaspoon sweet paprika
3 cups (750ml) water
1 litre (4 cups) vegetable stock
½ cup (125ml) pouring cream
2 teaspoons white (granulated) sugar
1 tablespoon finely chopped fresh chives

FRIED POLENTA
1 cup (170g) instant polenta
3½ cups (875ml) water
20g (¾ ounce) butter
1 cup (80g) finely grated parmesan
vegetable oil, to shallow-fry

1 Make fried polenta fingers.
2 Preheat grill (broiler). Quarter capsicums, discard seeds and membranes. Roast garlic and capsicum under hot grill, skin-side up, until skin blisters and blackens. Cover capsicum with plastic wrap for 5 minutes, peel away skin. Peel garlic; chop coarsely.
3 Heat oil in a large saucepan over medium heat; cook onion, stirring, until softened. Add paprika; cook, stirring, until fragrant.
4 Add the water, stock, capsicum and garlic to pan; bring to the boil. Reduce heat; simmer, uncovered, for 40 minutes. Cool 10 minutes.
5 Blend or process soup, in batches, until smooth. Return soup to pan, add cream and sugar; stir over medium heat until hot. Season.
6 Sprinkle soup with chives; accompany with polenta fingers.

FRIED POLENTA Cook polenta and the water following packet directions. Stir in butter and parmesan. Spoon into a baking-paper-lined 20cm x 30cm (8-inch x 12-inch) slice pan. Refrigerate until set. Just before serving, turn out onto a board; cut into 18 fingers. Heat oil in a large frying pan until hot. Shallow-fry, in batches, until polenta fingers are golden.

nutritional count per serving 39g total fat
(12.4g saturated fat); 1796kJ (429 cal);
27.5g carbohydrate; 10.9g protein; 4.1g fibre

notes Soup is suitable to freeze.
Instead of the fried polenta, serve soup with
fresh crusty sourdough breadrolls.

CREAMY PUMPKIN & POTATO SOUP

prep + cook time 35 minutes serves 4

1 tablespoon olive oil

1 medium brown onion (150g), chopped coarsely

1 clove garlic, crushed

600g (1¼ pounds) pumpkin, chopped coarsely

2 medium potatoes (400g), chopped coarsely

2 cups (500ml) water

1½ cups (375ml) vegetable stock

½ cup (125ml) pouring cream

1 tablespoon lemon juice

GARLIC & CHIVE CROÛTONS

⅓ loaf ciabatta (150g)

2 tablespoons olive oil

1 clove garlic, crushed

1 tablespoon finely chopped fresh chives

1 Heat oil in a large saucepan over medium heat; cook onion and garlic, stirring, 5 minutes or until onion softens. Add pumpkin, potato, the water and stock; bring to the boil. Reduce heat; simmer, covered, 20 minutes or until vegetables are tender. Cool 10 minutes.

2 Meanwhile, make garlic and chive croûtons.

3 Blend or process soup, in batches, until smooth. Return soup to pan; add cream and juice. Reheat, stirring, until hot (do not reboil soup).

4 Serve soup topped with croûtons.

GARLIC & CHIVE CROÛTONS Preheat oven to 180°C/350°F. Cut bread into 2cm (¾-inch) cubes; combine in a large bowl with oil, garlic and chives. Place bread on an oven tray; bake, turning occasionally, 12 minutes or until golden.

nutritional count per serving 29.3g total fat (11.7g saturated fat); 2006kJ (480 cal); 41.4g carbohydrate; 10.7g protein; 5g fibre

notes Recipe is suitable to freeze. Fresh sage and thyme also go well with pumpkin. Top with shavings of parmesan, if you like.

POTATO SOUP WITH CAPSICUM & ALMONDS

prep + cook time 40 minutes **serves** 4

1 tablespoon extra virgin olive oil
2 medium brown onions (300g),
  chopped finely
4 cloves garlic, crushed
pinch saffron threads
5 medium potatoes (1kg), chopped coarsely
3 cups (750ml) vegetable stock
3 cups (750ml) water
2 tablespoons blanched almonds
⅔ cup (150g) capsicum (bell pepper) dip

1 Heat oil in a large saucepan over medium heat; cook onion, stirring, until soft. Add garlic and saffron; cook, stirring, until fragrant.
2 Add potato to the pan with stock and the water; simmer, covered, 20 minutes or until soft. Stand 10 minutes.
3 Meanwhile, dry-fry nuts in a small frying pan over medium heat until browned lightly. Remove from pan immediately to stop from over-browning; cool, then chop coarsely.
4 Blend or process soup, in batches, until smooth. Return soup to pan; stir over medium heat until hot. Season to taste.
5 Ladle soup into serving bowls; top with dip, nuts and freshly ground black pepper.

nutritional count per serving 11.8g total fat
(3.3g saturated fat); 1235kJ (295 cal);
33.3g carbohydrate; 10.1g protein; 6.7g fibre

notes Recipe is suitable to freeze.
Starchy potatoes, such as sebago, are best to use.
Reheat before topping with dip and almonds.

BARLEY & VEGETABLE SOUP WITH CRUNCHY SEEDS

prep + cook time 45 minutes **serves** 6

2 tablespoons extra virgin olive oil

1 large red onion (300g), chopped coarsely

1 medium parsnip (250g), chopped coarsely

2 stalks celery (300g), trimmed,
  chopped coarsely

4 cloves garlic, chopped finely

1 cup (250ml) bottled tomato pasta sauce
  (passata)

1 litre (4 cups) vegetable stock

1 litre (4 cups) water

2 medium red capsicums (bell peppers)
  (400g), chopped coarsely

400g (12½ ounces) canned cannellini
  beans, rinsed, drained

½ cup (100g) pearl barley or spelt,
  rinsed, drained

2 tablespoons pepitas (pumpkin seeds)

2 tablespoons sunflower seeds

2 tablespoons rinsed, drained baby capers

2 tablespoons dried currants

¼ cup loosely packed torn fresh basil leaves

½ cup (40g) finely grated parmesan

1 Heat half the oil in a large saucepan over medium heat; cook onion, parsnip, celery and garlic, stirring, 5 minutes or until softened.

2 Add sauce, stock and the water; bring to the boil. Stir in capsicum, beans and barley; simmer, covered, 25 minutes or until barley is tender. Season to taste.

3 Meanwhile, heat remaining oil in a small frying pan over medium heat; cook pepitas, seeds and capers, stirring, until browned lightly and fragrant. Stir in currants.

4 Just before serving, stir basil into soup. Ladle soup into serving bowls; sprinkle with seed mixture and parmesan.

nutritional count per serving 11.1g total fat (2.7g saturated fat); 1244kJ (298 cal); 34.2g carbohydrate; 11.8g protein; 9.2g fibre

notes This soup, without the seed topping and parmesan, can be frozen for up to 3 months. Add a little extra water on reheating, if needed.

SPICED CARROT SOUP WITH SMOKED ALMONDS

prep + cook time 40 minutes **serves** 4

1 tablespoon extra virgin olive oil

2 medium brown onions (300g), chopped coarsely

4cm (1½-inch) piece fresh ginger (20g), grated finely

2 teaspoons ground cumin

1 teaspoon ground coriander

½ cinnamon stick

1kg (2 pounds) carrots, cut into 1cm (½-inch) slices

2 cups (500ml) vegetable stock

3 cups (750ml) water

¾ cup (200g) greek-style yoghurt

2 cloves garlic, crushed

½ small red onion (50g), sliced thinly lengthways

¼ cup (40g) coarsely chopped smoked almonds

8 sprigs fresh coriander (cilantro)

1 Heat oil in a large saucepan over medium heat; cook brown onion, stirring, until soft.

2 Add ginger and spices to pan; cook, stirring, until fragrant. Add carrot, stock and the water; bring to the boil. Reduce heat; simmer, covered, 20 minutes or until soft. Discard cinnamon stick. Cool soup 10 minutes.

3 Blend soup, in batches, until smooth. Return soup to pan; stir over medium heat until hot. Season to taste.

4 Meanwhile, combine yoghurt and garlic in a small bowl.

5 Top soup with yoghurt mixture, red onion, nuts and fresh coriander, to serve.

nutritional count per serving 14.5g total fat (3.3g saturated fat); 1190kJ (284 cal); 24g carbohydrate; 8.9g protein; 11.7g fibre

notes Recipe is suitable to freeze at the end of step 3. Thaw overnight in the fridge before continuing from step 4.

CREAM OF ZUCCHINI SOUP

prep + cook time 35 minutes **serves** 4

30g (1 ounce) butter
1 large brown onion (200g), chopped finely
2 cloves garlic, crushed
2 tablespoons plain (all-purpose) flour
8 large zucchini (1.2kg), chopped coarsely
1½ cups (375ml) vegetable stock
1 cup (250ml) water
½ cup (125ml) pouring cream
1 tablespoon pouring cream, extra
1 tablespoon coarsely chopped fresh chives

1 Melt butter in a large saucepan over medium heat; cook onion and garlic, stirring, until onion softens. Add flour and zucchini; cook, stirring, 2 minutes.

2 Stir in stock and the water; bring to the boil. Reduce heat; simmer, uncovered, for 15 minutes or until zucchini is tender. Cool 10 minutes.

3 Blend or process soup, in batches, until smooth.

4 Just before serving, return soup to pan. Add cream; stir over medium heat until hot. Season to taste. To serve, drizzle with extra cream and sprinkle with chives.

nutritional count per serving 20.6g total fat (12.5g saturated fat); 1111kJ (265 cal); 12.9g carbohydrate; 5.5g protein; 5.1g fibre

notes Recipe is not suitable to freeze. Don't reboil the soup once you add the cream, as the soup may curdle.

VEGETABLE HARIRA SOUP

prep + cook time 2 hours (+ standing) **serves** 6

1 cup (200g) dried chickpeas
 (garbanzo beans)
large pinch saffron threads
2kg (4 pounds) ripe tomatoes
2 tablespoons olive oil
2 medium brown onions (340g),
 chopped coarsely
2 stalks celery (300g), trimmed,
 chopped coarsely
1½ teaspoons ground cinnamon
1 teaspoon each ground turmeric and ginger
1.25 litres (5 cups) water
1 cup (200g) french-style green lentils
½ cup coarsely chopped fresh flat-leaf
 parsley
½ cup coarsely chopped fresh coriander
 (cilantro)

1 Stand chickpeas overnight in a medium bowl of cold water. Drain; rinse well.
2 Place saffron in a small bowl with 1 tablespoon water.
3 Cut a shallow cross in the base of tomatoes; place in a large bowl. Cover with boiling water, stand for 30 seconds; drain. Remove skins and discard; puree flesh in a blender.
4 Heat oil in a large saucepan over medium heat; cook onion, celery, spices and saffron with soaking liquid, stirring, for 5 minutes or until vegetables have softened. Add tomato, the water and chickpeas; bring to the boil. Skim off any scum that rises to the surface. Reduce heat to low; simmer, partially covered, for 45 minutes. Add lentils; simmer, partially covered, for 45 minutes or until lentils and chickpeas are tender. Season with salt.
5 Stir half the herbs through soup. Divide soup among bowls; serve topped with remaining herbs. Accompany with fresh crusty bread rolls, if you like.

nutritional count per serving 14.1g total fat (2g saturated fat); 1516kJ (362 cal); 28.4g carbohydrate; 23.4g protein; 17.9g fibre

note Harira, a Moroccan soup traditionally made with lamb, vegetables and pulses, is served to break the fast of Ramadan.

LENTIL & VEGETABLE SOUP

prep + cook time 1 hour **serves** 2

2 stalks celery (300g)
2 litres (8 cups) vegetable stock
1 cup (200g) french-style green lentils
2 cloves garlic, crushed
2 large carrots (360g), chopped coarsely
200g (6 ounces) mushrooms,
   chopped coarsely
⅓ cup coarsely chopped fresh
   flat-leaf parsley

1 Trim celery stalk, reserving the celery leaves. Coarsely chop celery stalk. Combine stock, lentils, garlic and celery leaves in a medium saucepan; bring to the boil. Reduce heat; simmer, covered, for 20 minutes or until lentils just soften. Discard celery leaves.
2 Add chopped celery stalk, carrot and mushrooms; bring to the boil. Reduce heat; simmer, covered, 15 minutes or until vegetables are tender. Stir in parsley. Season to taste.

nutritional count per serving 1.7g total fat (0.2g saturated fat); 978kJ (234 cal); 37.5g carbohydrate; 18g protein; 17.7g fibre

notes Recipe is not suitable to freeze. Button, swiss brown or portobello mushrooms, or a mixture, are all suitable to use here.

POTATO & LEEK SOUP

prep + cook time 1½ hours (+ cooling) **serves** 4

2 medium potatoes (400g), chopped coarsely
2 medium carrots (240g), chopped coarsely
1 large brown onion (200g), chopped coarsely
1 medium tomato (150g), chopped coarsely
1 stalk celery (150g), trimmed, chopped
  coarsely
1.5 litres (6 cups) water
1 tablespoon olive oil
50g (1½ ounces) butter
4 medium potatoes (800g), chopped coarsely,
  extra
1 large leek (500g), sliced thickly
300ml pouring cream
2 tablespoons finely chopped fresh chives
1 tablespoon each finely chopped fresh
  basil and dill

1 Place potato, carrot, onion, tomato, celery and the water in a large saucepan; bring to the boil. Reduce heat; simmer, uncovered, for 25 minutes. Strain broth through a muslin-lined sieve or colander into a large heatproof bowl; discard solids.
2 Heat oil and butter in same pan over medium heat; cook extra potato and leek, covered, for 20 minutes, stirring occasionally. Add broth; bring to the boil. Reduce heat; simmer, covered, for 15 minutes. Cool 15 minutes.
3 Blend or process soup, in batches, until smooth.
4 Return soup to pan, add cream; stir over medium heat until hot. Season to taste.
5 Serve soup sprinkled with combined herbs and, if you like, topped with croûtons.

nutritional count per serving 46.9g total fat (28.1g saturated fat); 2812kJ (665 cal); 46.3g carbohydrate; 11g protein; 9.8g fibre

notes Recipe is suitable to freeze at the end of step 3. Thaw overnight in the fridge. Reheat and continue recipe from step 4.

SOUPE AU PISTOU

prep + cook time 35 minutes **serves** 4

1 tablespoon olive oil

1 small brown onion (80g), chopped finely

2 cloves garlic, sliced thinly

1 large carrot (180g), chopped finely

1 stalk celery (150g), trimmed,
   chopped finely

1 medium potato (200g), cut into 1cm
   (½-inch) cubes

⅓ cup (75g) risoni pasta

3 cups (750ml) vegetable stock

1 cup (250ml) water

400g (12½ ounces) canned white beans,
   rinsed, drained

2 tablespoons lemon juice

⅓ cup (90g) basil pesto

1 Heat oil in a large saucepan over medium heat; cook onion, garlic, carrot and celery, stirring, until onion softens. Add potato, pasta, stock and the water; bring to the boil. Reduce heat; simmer 10 minutes or until pasta is tender.

2 Stir in beans; simmer, uncovered, for 1 minute. Remove from heat; stir in juice. Season to taste. Serve with basil pesto.

nutritional count per serving 13.5g total fat (2.2g saturated fat); 1209kJ (289 cal); 11.7g carbohydrate; 27.8g protein; 6.9g fibre

notes Recipe is not suitable to freeze. Any white beans, such as cannellini, haricot, navy or great northern beans, can be used here.

ONION AND FENNEL SOUP WITH CHEESE SOUFFLÉS

prep + cook time 1 hour (+ cooling) **serves** 6

60g (2 ounces) butter
1kg (2 pounds) brown onions, sliced thinly
1 medium fennel (300g), sliced thinly
1 teaspoon fresh thyme leaves
1 teaspoon brown sugar
1 litre (4 cups) vegetable stock
2 cups (500ml) water

CHEESE SOUFFLÉS
50g (1½ ounces) butter, chopped
⅓ cup (50g) plain (all-purpose) flour
1½ cups (375ml) milk
1 cup (120g) coarsely grated vintage cheddar
3 eggs, separated
⅓ cup (80ml) pouring cream

1 Heat butter in a large saucepan over medium heat; cook onion, fennel and thyme, covered, 20 minutes or until very soft. Add sugar; cook, stirring occasionally, 20 minutes or until onion and fennel are caramelised.
2 Meanwhile, make cheese soufflés.
3 Stir stock and the water into onion mixture; bring to the boil. Reduce heat; simmer, covered, 5 minutes. Season to taste.
4 Place soufflés in serving bowls; pour soup around soufflés. Sprinkle with extra thyme.

CHEESE SOUFFLÉS Preheat oven to 180°C/350°F. Grease six ⅔ cup (160ml) metal dariole moulds or soufflé dishes; line bases with baking paper. Melt butter in a medium saucepan over medium heat, add flour; cook, stirring, 1 minute. Gradually stir in milk; stir until mixture boils and thickens. Transfer mixture to a medium heatproof bowl. Stir in ¾ cup of the cheddar, then egg yolks. Season to taste. Beat egg whites in a small bowl with an electric mixer until soft peaks form. Fold egg white into cheese mixture, in two batches. Spoon mixture into dishes. Place dishes in a small baking dish; add enough boiling water to the baking dish to come halfway up side of the dishes. Bake soufflés 15 minutes or until firm. Cool soufflés 5 minutes; turn soufflés out onto a baking-paper-lined ovenproof dish. Cool. Spoon cream over soufflés; top with remaining cheddar. Bake a further 15 minutes or until puffed and browned.

nutritional count per serving 32.6g total fat (16.7g saturated fat); 1852kJ (442 cal); 20.4g carbohydrate; 16.4g protein; 4g fibre

notes The soup can be made a day ahead. The soufflés can be baked the first time 8 hours ahead. Bake for the second time just before serving.

311

PUMPKIN &
EGGPLANT LAKSA

prep + cook time 1 hour **serves** 6

700g (1½-pound) piece butternut pumpkin,
  diced into 2cm (¾-inch) pieces
5 baby eggplants (300g), sliced thickly
3 cups (750ml) vegetable stock
1⅔ cups (400ml) coconut milk
250g (8 ounces) rice stick noodles
500g (1 pound) buk choy, chopped coarsely
2 tablespoons lime juice
1¼ cups (100g) bean sprouts
6 green onions (scallions), sliced thinly
½ cup fresh coriander leaves (cilantro)
½ cup vietnamese mint leaves

LAKSA PASTE
7 medium dried red chillies
½ cup (125ml) boiling water
1 tablespoon peanut oil
3 cloves garlic, quartered
1 medium brown onion (150g), chopped
10cm (4-inch) stick fresh lemon grass
  (20g), chopped finely
4cm (1½-inch) piece fresh ginger (20g),
  grated
1 tablespoon halved macadamias
1 fresh coriander (cilantro) root, washed,
  chopped coarsely
1 teaspoon each ground turmeric and
  coriander
2 teaspoons salt
¼ cup loosely packed vietnamese mint leaves

1 Make laksa paste.
2 Place ½ cup of the paste in a large
saucepan over medium heat; cook, stirring,
until fragrant. Add pumpkin and eggplant;
cook, stirring, 2 minutes. Add stock and
coconut milk; bring to the boil. Reduce heat;
simmer, covered, 10 minutes or until
vegetables are tender.
3 Meanwhile, place noodles in a large
heatproof bowl, cover with boiling water,
stand until just tender; drain.
4 Stir buk choy into laksa; return to the boil.
Remove from heat; stir in juice. Season.
5 Divide noodles among serving bowls; ladle
laksa over noodles, sprinkle with combined
sprouts, onion and herbs.

LAKSA PASTE Cover chillies with the boiling
water in a small heatproof bowl, stand for
10 minutes; drain. Blend or process chillies
with remaining ingredients until mixture
forms a smooth paste. Measure ½ cup of
the paste for this recipe; freeze remaining
paste, covered, for future use.

---

nutritional count per serving 20.7g total fat
(13.3g saturated fat); 1405kJ; (336 cal);
25.8g carbohydrate; 7.9g protein; 8.4g fibre

notes Recipe is not suitable to freeze.
Keep the roots from the bunch of fresh coriander
as they are used in the laksa paste.

CREAM OF BEETROOT SOUP WITH DUMPLINGS

prep + cook time 1¼ hours (+ cooling) **serves** 4

30g (1 ounce) butter
1 tablespoon olive oil
1 large brown onion (200g), chopped coarsely
2 cloves garlic, crushed
1 teaspoon sweet paprika
½ cup (125ml) dry white wine
5 medium beetroot (beets) (1.5kg),
   trimmed, peeled, chopped coarsely
1 litre (4 cups) vegetable stock
¾ cup (180ml) pouring cream
2 tablespoons coarsely chopped fresh chives

DUMPLINGS
110g (3½ ounces) crumbled goat's cheese
2 egg yolks
⅓ cup (50g) self-raising flour
⅓ cup (25g) finely grated parmesan
1 tablespoon finely chopped fresh chives

1 Heat butter and oil in a large saucepan over medium heat; cook onion and garlic, stirring, until onion softens. Add paprika; cook, stirring, until fragrant. Add wine; simmer, uncovered, about 2 minutes or until reduced by half.

2 Add beetroot and stock to pan; bring to the boil. Reduce heat; simmer, uncovered, stirring occasionally, about 40 minutes or until beetroot softens. Cool 15 minutes.
3 Meanwhile, make dumplings.
4 Blend or process soup, in batches, until smooth. Return soup to pan, add cream; stir over medium heat until hot. Season to taste.
5 Serve soup topped with dumplings and sprinkled with chives.

DUMPLINGS Combine cheese, egg yolks, flour, parmesan and chives in a small bowl; season. Drop level tablespoons of mixture into a large saucepan of simmering water; cook, uncovered, 5 minutes or until dumplings are cooked through. Remove using slotted spoon; drain on absorbent paper.

nutritional count per serving 39.5g total fat (21.5g saturated fat); 2639kJ (630 cal); 40.5g carbohydrate; 20.3g protein; 13.4g fibre

notes Fetta cheese can be used instead of the goat's cheese. Dollop some sour cream on top of the soup before serving, if you like.

CREAMY FRESH TOMATO SOUP

prep + cook time 1¼ hours (+ cooling) **serves** 6

1.3kg (2¾ pounds) large tomatoes, quartered

2 tablespoons olive oil

2 tablespoons brown sugar

1 medium brown onion (150g),
   chopped coarsely

2 cloves garlic, crushed

2 cups (500ml) vegetable stock

810g (1½ pounds) canned crushed tomatoes

1½ cups (375ml) pouring cream

½ cup (125ml) thick (double) cream

2 tablespoons coarsely chopped fresh chives

CHEESE CROÛTONS

1 small french bread stick (150g),
   sliced thickly

1 cup (120g) coarsely grated cheddar

½ cup (40g) coarsely grated parmesan

1 Preheat oven to 200°C/400°F.

2 Combine quartered tomatoes, half the oil and all the sugar in a medium shallow baking dish; season. Roast 30 minutes or until softened. Cool 20 minutes; peel tomatoes, discard skin.

3 Meanwhile, heat remaining oil in a large saucepan over medium heat; cook onion and garlic, stirring, until onion softens. Add stock, canned tomatoes and roasted tomatoes to pan; bring to the boil. Reduce heat; simmer, uncovered, 15 minutes. Cool 20 minutes.

4 Meanwhile, make cheese croûtons.

5 Blend or process soup, in batches, until smooth. Strain soup back into pan; discard solids. Add pouring cream; stir over heat, without boiling, until soup is heated through. Season to taste.

6 Top soup with thickened cream; sprinkle with chives and accompany with croûtons to serve.

CHEESE CROÛTONS Preheat grill (broiler). Toast bread on one side then turn and sprinkle with combined cheeses; grill croûtons until cheese melts and browns lightly.

---

nutritional count per serving 51.6g total fat (29.7g saturated fat); 2748kJ (656 cal); 30.4g carbohydrate; 16.1g protein; 5.7g fibre

notes Recipe is not suitable to freeze. Use in-season vine-ripened tomatoes when making this soup for a fuller tomato flavour.

BEAN & BASIL SOUP

prep + cook time 30 minutes serves 4

1 tablespoon extra virgin olive oil

1 medium brown onion (150g), chopped finely

3 cloves garlic, crushed

1 litre (4 cups) vegetable stock

1 cup (250ml) water

800g (1½ pounds) canned butter beans, rinsed, drained

250g (8 ounces) green beans, halved

2 large zucchini (300g), halved lengthways, sliced thickly crossways

½ cup (40g) shaved parmesan

2 tablespoons basil pesto

1 Heat oil in a large saucepan over medium heat; cook onion, stirring, until softened. Add garlic; cook, stirring, until fragrant. Stir in stock and the water; bring to the boil. Add butter beans; simmer, covered, 10 minutes.

2 Add green beans and zucchini to soup; simmer, covered, 5 minutes or until vegetables are just tender. Season to taste. Sprinkle soup with cheese; accompany with pesto.

nutritional count per serving 13.7g total fat (3.9g saturated fat); 1275kJ (305 cal); 24.3g carbohydrate; 17.4g protein; 12.8g fibre

notes Recipe is not suitable to freeze. Butter beans are also known as lima beans; you can use cannellini or similar white beans.

CURRIED VEGETABLE & LENTIL SOUP

prep + cook time 30 minutes **serves** 6

1 litre (4 cups) vegetable stock

1 litre (4 cups) water

500g (1 pound) butternut pumpkin, peeled, chopped finely

2 teaspoons olive oil

1 medium brown onion (170g), chopped finely

1 large clove garlic, crushed

1 medium carrot (120g), chopped finely

1 stalk celery (150g), trimmed, chopped finely

3 teaspoons curry powder

1 cup (120g) frozen peas

400g (12½ ounces) canned brown lentils, rinsed, drained

¼ cup (60ml) lemon juice

¼ cup loosely packed fresh coriander leaves (cilantro)

1 Place stock, the water and pumpkin in a medium saucepan, cover; bring to the boil. Reduce heat; simmer, uncovered, about 5 minutes or until pumpkin is almost tender.

2 Meanwhile, heat oil in a large saucepan over high heat; cook onion, garlic, carrot and celery, stirring, until softened. Add curry powder; stir until fragrant. Add pumpkin mixture and peas to pan; simmer about 10 minutes or until vegetables are tender. Stir in lentils and juice.

3 Serve soup sprinkled with coriander. Accompany with crusty bread, if you like.

nutritional count per serving 2.7g total fat (0.5g saturated fat); 530kJ (127 cal); 15.3g carbohydrate; 7.2g protein; 6.7g fibre

notes Recipe is not suitable to freeze. Curry powder is a blend of ground spices used for making curries; it comes as both mild and hot.

RATATOUILLE SOUP WITH PISTOU

prep + cook time 45 minutes serves 6

2 tablespoons extra virgin olive oil
2 medium red onions (340g),
   chopped coarsely
1 medium eggplant (300g),
   chopped coarsely
2 medium red capsicums (bell peppers)
   (400g), chopped coarsely
4 cloves garlic, chopped finely
2 medium green zucchini (240g),
   chopped coarsely
800g (1½ pounds) canned diced tomatoes
1 litre (4 cups) vegetable stock
2 x 110g (3½-ounce) mini french bread sticks
300g (9½ ounces) ricotta
½ cup (40g) finely grated parmesan

PISTOU
2 cloves garlic, peeled
¼ cup (60ml) extra virgin olive oil
1 cup loosely packed fresh basil leaves

1 Heat oil in a large saucepan over medium heat; cook onion, stirring, 5 minutes or until soft. Add eggplant, capsicum and garlic; cook, covered, over low heat, 20 minutes or until soft.
2 Add zucchini, tomatoes and stock; simmer, covered, 10 minutes or until zucchini is tender. Season to taste.
3 Meanwhile, make pistou.
4 Preheat grill (broiler).
5 Split bread lengthways, then in half crossways. Spread with 2 tablespoons of the pistou then ricotta; sprinkle with parmesan. Place on an oven tray under the grill until browned lightly.
6 Ladle soup into serving bowls; top with remaining pistou. Serve with bread.

PISTOU Blend or process ingredients until almost smooth; season to taste. Transfer to a small bowl; cover tightly with plastic wrap.

nutritional count per serving 23.3g total fat (6.5g saturated fat); 1759kJ (420 cal); 33.3g carbohydrate; 16.1g protein; 7.4g fibre

notes Recipe is not suitable to freeze. Pistou is the French version of Italian pesto, but without the parmesan and pine nuts.

WHITE MINESTRONE

prep + cook time 30 minutes **serves** 4

1 tablespoon extra virgin olive oil

1 large brown onion (200g), sliced thinly

2 cloves garlic, crushed

1 large fennel bulb (550g), sliced thinly, reserve fronds

¼ small cabbage (300g), sliced thinly

3 cups (750ml) vegetable stock

3 cups (750ml) water

2 cups (160g) dried fusilli pasta

400g (12½ ounces) canned cannellini beans, rinsed, drained

½ cup (60g) frozen peas

1 cup (80g) finely grated parmesan

⅓ cup (90g) basil pesto

¼ cup (25g) flaked parmesan

1 Heat oil in a large saucepan over medium heat; cook onion, garlic and fennel, stirring, until softened. Add cabbage, stock and the water; bring to the boil. Reduce heat; simmer, uncovered, 10 minutes. Add pasta; cook, stirring occasionally, until tender.

2 Add beans, peas and grated cheese to pan; cook, stirring occasionally, about 5 minutes or until heated through. Season to taste.

3 Serve soup topped with pesto, flaked cheese and reserved fennel fronds.

nutritional count per serving 23.7g total fat (7.8g saturated fat); 2277kJ (544 cal); 53.3g carbohydrate; 26.1g protein; 7.1g fibre

notes Recipe is not suitable to freeze. Fusilli are long, thick corkscrew (spiral) shaped pasta; use any spiral pasta you like.

ROOT VEGETABLE SOUP WITH CHEESY TOASTS

prep + cook time 30 minutes **serves** 4

2 medium carrots (240g), chopped coarsely

2 stalks celery (300g), trimmed, chopped coarsely

1 large parsnip (350g), chopped coarsely

2 medium potatoes (400g), chopped coarsely

4cm (1½-inch) piece fresh ginger (30g), chopped coarsely

50g (1½ ounces) butter

¼ cup loosely packed fresh sage leaves

2 teaspoons honey

3½ cups (875ml) vegetable stock

½ cup (125ml) pouring cream

2 tablespoons finely chopped fresh chives

CHEESY TOASTS

1 small brioche loaf (360g)

⅓ cup (25g) flaked parmesan

1 Blend or process chopped vegetables with the ginger, in batches, until finely chopped.

2 Melt butter in a large saucepan over medium heat; cook sage about 1 minute or until fragrant. Add vegetable mixture to pan; cook, stirring, until softened. Add honey to pan; cook, stirring, until vegetables are golden. Stir in stock; bring to the boil. Reduce heat; simmer, covered, 15 minutes or until vegetables are soft. Cool 10 minutes.

3 Meanwhile, make cheesy toasts.

4 Blend or process soup, in batches, until smooth. Return soup to pan; add cream, stir until heated through. Season to taste.

5 Sprinkle soup with chives; drizzle over a little extra cream, if you like. Serve with cheesy toasts.

CHEESY TOASTS Preheat grill (broiler). Thinly slice brioche into 12 slices. Toast one side of brioche slices under grill; turn, sprinkle with cheese. Grill until browned lightly.

nutritional count per serving 25.8g total fat (15.7g saturated fat); 2231kJ (533 cal); 59.7g carbohydrate; 12g protein; 8.3g fibre

notes Recipe is not suitable to freeze. Any bread is suitable to use for the cheesy toasts. Try a sourdough loaf if you can't find brioche.

TOM YUM SOUP

prep + cook time 40 minutes **serves** 4

You will need about 3 limes for this recipe. Grate the rind from the limes before juicing.

2 tablespoons vegetable oil
1 tablespoon finely grated fresh ginger
1 clove garlic, crushed
2 x 20cm (8-inch) sticks lemon grass (40g), chopped finely
2 fresh long red chillies, chopped finely
100g (3 ounces) fresh shiitake mushrooms, sliced thickly
125g (4 ounces) cherry tomatoes, halved
2 green onions (scallions), sliced thinly
2 teaspoons finely grated palm sugar
¼ cup (60ml) soy sauce
¼ cup (60ml) lime juice
2 cups (160g) bean sprouts
¼ cup loosely packed fresh coriander leaves (cilantro)

STOCK
1 fresh long red chilli, sliced thinly
2 green onions (scallions), sliced thinly
1 cup lightly packed fresh coriander leaves (cilantro), sliced thinly
1 tablespoon finely grated fresh ginger
6 fresh kaffir lime leaves, torn
2 tablespoons tomato paste
1 tablespoon finely grated lime rind
2 litres (8 cups) water
2 cups (500ml) vegetable stock

1 Make the stock.

2 Heat oil in a large saucepan over medium heat; cook ginger, garlic, lemon grass and half the chilli, stirring, 3 minutes or until fragrant. Add mushrooms; cook, stirring, 2 minutes.

3 Stir in stock, tomato, onion, sugar and sauce; bring to the boil. Reduce heat; simmer 5 minutes.

4 Just before serving, stir in juice. Ladle soup into serving bowls; top with combined bean sprouts, coriander and remaining chilli.

STOCK Place ingredients in a large saucepan; bring to the boil. Reduce heat; simmer, uncovered, 20 minutes (use a large ladle to skim any scum from the surface of the stock). Remove from heat. Strain stock through a fine sieve into a heatproof jug or bowl; discard the solids. You need 3 litres (12 cups) of stock.

nutritional count per serving 10.3g total fat (1.3g saturated fat); 603kJ (144 cal); 7g carbohydrate; 4.8g protein; 2.9g fibre

notes Recipe is not suitable to freeze. This is our vegetarian take on Thailand's popular hot and spicy prawn soup.

WHITE GAZPACHO

prep time 25 minutes (+ standing) **serves** 6

White gazpacho is a variation to the more well-known chilled tomato-based gazpacho. It reflects the Moorish influence of southern Spain – the use of ground almonds and freshly chopped herbs in a soup is more North African than Spanish. Ground almonds (sometimes sold as almond meal), as the name suggests, is a coarse flour made by pulverising almonds.

6 slices white bread (270g)
2 tablespoons sherry vinegar
3 cups (750ml) water
1½ cups (180g) ground almonds
2 tablespoons coarsely chopped fresh chervil
2 lebanese cucumbers (260g), seeded, chopped finely
1 teaspoon salt
300ml pouring cream
1½ tablespoons extra virgin olive oil

1 Discard crusts from bread. Combine remaining bread in large glass bowl with vinegar and the water; stand 15 minutes. Whisk in ground almonds and half the chervil.
2 Meanwhile, place cucumber in a colander; sprinkle with salt, stand 15 minutes. Rinse cucumber under cold water; drain on absorbent paper.
3 Blend or process bread mixture and cream, in batches, until smooth. Return soup mixture to same bowl; stir in cucumber. [The gazpacho can be made ahead to this stage. Cover; refrigerate overnight.]
4 Season soup to taste; stir. Divide soup among serving bowls; drizzle with oil, sprinkle with remaining chervil.

nutritional count per serving 39.8g total fat (13.2g saturated fat); 1909kJ (456 cal); 14g carbohydrate; 9.6g protein; 3.9g fibre

notes Recipe is not suitable to freeze. You can substitute fresh mint leaves for chervil and red wine vinegar for the sherry vinegar.

MUSHROOM SOUP WITH HERBED CHEESE CROÛTES

prep + cook time 35 minutes **serves** 4

40g (1½ ounces) butter
1 tablespoon extra virgin olive oil
1 large brown onion (200g),
  chopped coarsely
200g (6½ ounces) swiss brown mushrooms,
  sliced thinly
500g (1 pound) cup mushrooms,
  sliced thinly
2 cloves garlic, crushed
1 teaspoon coarsely chopped fresh
  thyme leaves
1 litre (4 cups) vegetable stock
2 cups (500ml) water
100g (3 ounces) baby spinach leaves

HERBED GOAT'S CHEESE CROÛTES
8 thick slices sourdough bread (320g)
120g (4 ounces) soft goat's cheese
1 clove garlic, crushed
1 tablespoon coarsely chopped fresh chives
1 tablespoon coarsely chopped fresh
  flat-leaf parsley
1 teaspoon coarsely chopped fresh
  thyme leaves

1 Heat butter and oil in a large saucepan over medium heat. Add onion to pan; cook, stirring, 5 minutes or until onion is soft but not browned.
2 Increase heat to high. Add mushrooms to pan; cook, stirring, 5 minutes or until well browned. Add garlic and thyme; cook, stirring, until fragrant. Stir in stock and the water; simmer, covered, 15 minutes or until tender.
3 Meanwhile, make herbed cheese croûtes.
4 Add spinach to soup, stir until wilted. Season to taste.
5 Ladle soup into bowls; sprinkle with a few extra thyme sprigs. Serve with croûtes.

HERBED CHEESE CROÛTES Preheat grill (broiler). Place bread under grill until toasted lightly on both sides. Combine cheese, garlic and herbs in a small bowl; spread herbed cheese mixture on toast.

nutritional count per serving 23.1g total fat (10.9g saturated fat); 2082kJ (497 cal); 46.5g carbohydrate; 22.5g protein; 8.2g fibre

notes Recipe is not suitable to freeze. Button or portobello mushrooms can also be used in this recipe.

SLOW COOKER CAULIFLOWER SOUP

prep + cook time 7¼ hours **serves** 8

40g (1½ ounces) butter
2 large brown onions (400g),
   chopped coarsely
3 cloves garlic, crushed
1 litre (4 cups) vegetable stock
1 medium cauliflower (1.5kg), cut into florets
2 medium potatoes (400g), chopped coarsely
2 cups (500ml) water
300ml pouring cream
2 tablespoons finely chopped fresh
   flat-leaf parsley

1 Melt butter in a large frying pan over medium heat; cook onion, stirring, until softened. Add garlic to pan; cook, stirring, until fragrant. Add stock; bring to the boil.

2 Transfer onion mixture to a 4.5-litre (18-cup) slow cooker with cauliflower, potato and the water. Cook, covered, on low, for 6½ hours.

3 Blend or process soup, in batches, until smooth.

4 Return to cooker; stir in cream. Cook, covered, on high, for 15 minutes or until soup is hot. Season to taste. Serve soup sprinkled with parsley.

nutritional count per serving 17.3g total fat (10.9g saturated fat); 1021kJ (244 cal); 114.9g carbohydrate; 6g protein; 4.1g fibre

notes Recipe is suitable to freeze at the end of step 3. Thaw in the fridge; reheat in a saucepan before adding the cream and stirring until hot.

ROASTED TOMATO AND WHITE BEAN SOUP

prep + cook time 1¼ hours **serves** 4

1kg (2 pounds) ripe roma (egg) tomatoes, quartered
1 medium red onion (170g), cut into wedges
6 cloves garlic, unpeeled
1 tablespoon pure maple syrup
½ cup (125ml) extra virgin olive oil
⅓ cup loosely packed sage leaves
400g (12½ ounces) canned cannellini beans, rinsed, drained
2 cups (500ml) water

1 Preheat oven to 200°C/400°F.

2 Place tomato, onion and garlic in a roasting pan. Combine maple syrup and half the oil in a bowl, season to taste; pour over vegetables, then toss to coat. Roast for 45 minutes or until the tomatoes are very soft and coloured at the edges.

3 Meanwhile, heat remaining oil in a small frying pan over medium heat; fry sage leaves, stirring, for 1½ minutes or until crisp. Remove with a slotted spoon; drain on absorbent paper. Reserve sage oil.

4 Peel roasted garlic. Blend garlic, onion, two-thirds of the tomato and two-thirds of the beans until smooth. Pour mixture into a large saucepan with the water and remaining beans; cook over medium heat, stirring occasionally until heated through. Season to taste.

5 Top soup with remaining tomatoes and crisp sage leaves; drizzle with sage oil.

nutritional count per serving 29g total fat (4.6g saturated fat); 1595kJ (381 cal); 18.9g carbohydrate; 7.6g protein; 8g fibre

notes Recipe is not suitable to freeze. Use in-season vine-ripened tomatoes when making this soup for a fuller tomato flavour.

CHINESE NOODLE, TOFU AND VEGETABLE SOUP

prep + cook time 20 minutes **serves** 4

1 litre (4 cups) vegetable stock
1 litre (4 cups) water
1 tablespoon finely grated fresh ginger
1 clove garlic, crushed
¼ cup (60ml) light soy sauce
1 teaspoon white (granulated) sugar
100g (3 ounces) fresh shiitake mushrooms
300g (9½ ounces) gai lan
450g (14½ ounces) fresh hokkien noodles
1 medium carrot (120g), cut into
    long thin strips
1 stalk celery (150g), trimmed, cut into
    long thin strips
300g (9½ ounces) silken tofu
½ teaspoon sesame oil
1 fresh long red chilli, sliced thinly
2 green onions (scallions), sliced thinly
pinch ground white pepper

1 Bring stock, the water, ginger, garlic, sauce and sugar to the boil in a large saucepan.
2 Discard stems from mushrooms; thinly slice caps. Separate gai lan stems and leaves.
3 Place noodles in a large heatproof bowl, cover with boiling water; separate with a fork, drain.
4 Add carrot, celery, mushrooms, gai lan stems and noodles to pan; simmer, uncovered, 2 minutes. Add gai lan leaves; simmer for 1 minute or until just tender.
5 Cut tofu into 1.5cm (¾-inch) cubes; add to soup with oil. Season to taste with a little extra soy sauce or salt. Remove from heat.
6 Ladle soup into serving bowls; top with chilli, onion and pepper.

nutritional count per serving 5.7g total fat (0.8g saturated fat); 1414kJ (338 cal); 50.4g carbohydrate; 18.4g protein; 6g fibre

notes Recipe is not suitable to freeze; make it just before serving. Use a vegetable peeler with a julienne blade to slice the carrot into thin strips.

339

CREAM OF CELERIAC SOUP

prep + cook time 1½ hours **serves** 8

2kg (4 pounds) celeriac (celery root),
chopped coarsely
1 medium brown onion (150g),
chopped coarsely
1 stalk celery (150g), trimmed
chopped coarsely
3 cloves garlic, quartered
1.5 litres (6 cups) water
1 litre (4 cups) vegetable stock
½ cup (125ml) pouring cream
2 tablespoons lemon juice
⅓ cup loosely packed fresh chervil leaves
1 tablespoon extra virgin olive oil

1 Place celeriac, onion, celery, garlic, the water and stock in a large saucepan; bring to the boil. Reduce heat; simmer, covered, 1 hour or until tender. Remove pan from heat; stand, uncovered, 10 minutes.

2 Blend or process soup, in batches, until smooth. Return soup to pan; stir in cream, over medium-high heat, until hot. Season; stir in juice.

3 Serve soup sprinkled with chervil and drizzled with oil.

nutritional count per serving 8.9g total fat (4.1g saturated fat); 705kJ (168 cal); 12.6g carbohydrate; 4.6g protein; 11.2g fibre

notes Recipe is suitable to freeze. Celeriac is a tuberous root with brown skin, white flesh and a celery-like flavour.

GREEK BUTTER BEAN SOUP WITH FETTA AND OLIVES

prep + cook time 30 minutes **serves** 6

2 tablespoons extra virgin olive oil

1 large brown onion (200g),
   chopped coarsely

2 medium carrots (240g), chopped coarsely

1 stalk celery (150g), trimmed,
   chopped coarsely

2 cloves garlic, crushed

800g (1½ pounds) canned diced tomatoes

1 litre (4 cups) vegetable stock

2 cups (500ml) water

800g (1½ pounds) canned butter beans,
   rinsed, drained

2 medium green zucchini (240g), halved
   lengthways, sliced thinly

1 teaspoon finely grated lemon rind

⅓ cup (50g) pitted black olives,
   chopped coarsely

100g (3 ounces) greek-style fetta

1 tablespoon fresh dill sprigs

1 Heat half the oil in a large saucepan over medium heat; cook onion, carrot and celery, stirring, 5 minutes or until softened. Add garlic; cook, stirring, until fragrant.

2 Add tomatoes to pan with stock and the water; bring to the boil. Add beans; simmer, covered, 10 minutes. Add zucchini; simmer, uncovered, about 5 minutes or until tender. Stir in rind; season to taste.

3 Ladle soup into serving bowls; top with olives, crumbled fetta and dill. Drizzle with remaining oil. Accompany with warm pitta or crusty bread, if you like.

nutritional count per serving 9.7g total fat (3.4g saturated fat); 815kJ (195 cal); 14.1g carbohydrate; 9.1g protein; 7.2g fibre

notes Soup can be frozen at the end of step 2. Large canned butter beans are also known as lima beans; any white beans can be used.

CURRIED KUMARA AND LENTIL SOUP

prep + cook time 35 minutes **serves** 4

½ cup (100g) red lentils
1 tablespoon vegetable oil
1 large brown onion (200g), chopped coarsely
1 teaspoon cumin seeds
1 teaspoon brown mustard seeds
¼ cup (75g) madras curry paste
6 curry leaves
2 cups (500ml) coconut cream
1 litre (4 cups) vegetable stock
1 cup (250ml) water
1kg (2 pounds) kumara (orange sweet potato),
    cut into 1.5cm (¾-inch) pieces
¼ cup loosely packed fresh coriander sprigs
    (cilantro)
¼ cup loosely packed fresh mint leaves, torn
lemon wedges, to serve

1 Place lentils in a medium bowl; cover with cold water, stir well. Discard any lentils that float to the surface. Drain well.

2 Heat oil in a large saucepan over medium heat; cook onion, stirring, until soft. Add seeds, paste and leaves; cook, stirring, until fragrant.

3 Reserve 2 tablespoons coconut cream. Stir remaining coconut cream into the pan with stock and the water; bring to the boil.

4 Add kumara to pan; simmer, covered, 10 minutes. Add lentils; simmer, covered, a further 10 minutes or until tender. Season to taste. Remove curry leaves. Break up most of the kumara with a wooden spoon.

5 Ladle soup into serving bowls; top with reserved coconut cream, coriander sprigs and mint. Serve with lemon wedges and accompany with pappadums or chapatti, if you like.

nutritional count per serving 35.8g total fat (23.1g saturated fat); 2542kJ (607 cal); 51.9g carbohydrate; 16.1g protein; 11.2g fibre

notes Recipe is not suitable to freeze. Lentils that float to the surface when covered with water are usually old; it's best to discard them.

CAULIFLOWER, POTATO & BEAN SOUP

prep + cook time 45 minutes **serves** 4

1 tablespoon olive oil

1 medium brown onion (150g), chopped finely

1 litre (4 cups) water

1 litre (4 cups) vegetable stock

4 medium potatoes (800g), quartered

500g (1 pound) cauliflower, chopped coarsely

2 tablespoons tomato paste

3 cups (450g) frozen broad (fava) beans, thawed, peeled

2 eggs, beaten lightly

¼ cup (20g) finely grated parmesan

2 tablespoons finely chopped fresh mint

1 Heat oil in a large saucepan over medium heat; cook onion, stirring, until soft.

2 Add the water, stock, potato, cauliflower and paste to pan; bring to the boil. Reduce heat; simmer, uncovered, about 20 minutes or until vegetables are tender.

3 Remove from heat, add beans, egg and parmesan; cover, stand 5 minutes. Season to taste. Serve soup sprinkled with mint.

nutritional count per serving 10.6g total fat (2.8g saturated fat); 1433kJ (342 cal); 33.8g carbohydrate; 20.4g protein; 13.3g fibre

notes Recipe is not suitable to freeze. Broad beans have a tough beige-green inner covering that needs to be discarded.

SPICY TOMATO & CAPSICUM SOUP

prep + cook time 50 minutes serves 4

2 teaspoons olive oil
1 medium brown onion (150g), chopped finely
½ teaspoon dried chilli flakes
1 clove garlic, crushed
410g (13 ounces) canned tomato puree
5 medium tomatoes (750g), chopped finely
1⅓ cups (285g) drained char-grilled capsicum (bell pepper) in oil
2 medium potatoes (400g), chopped coarsely
1 litre (4 cups) vegetable stock
400g (12½ ounces) canned cannellini beans, rinsed, drained

1 Heat oil in a large saucepan over medium heat; cook onion, chilli and garlic, stirring, until onion softens. Add puree, tomato and capsicum; cook, stirring, 1 minute or until tomato softens.

2 Add potato and half the stock to pan; bring to the boil. Reduce heat; simmer, covered, 25 minutes or until potato is tender. Cool 10 minutes.

3 Blend or process soup until smooth. Return soup to pan with remaining stock and beans; stir over medium heat until heated through. Season to taste.

nutritional count per serving 8.9g total fat (1g saturated fat); 1019kJ (243 cal); 32.7g carbohydrate; 11g protein; 8.2g fibre

notes Recipe is not suitable to freeze. Use any white beans in place of the cannellini beans; try navy, butter or haricot beans.

ROASTED JERUSALEM ARTICHOKE SOUP

prep + cook time 1½ hours (+ standing) **serves** 4

650g (1¼ pounds) jerusalem artichokes
  (sunchokes)
¼ cup (60ml) olive oil
350g (11 ounces) baby leeks, sliced thinly
1 stalk celery (150g), trimmed, sliced thinly
1½ tablespoons tomato paste
1 large potato (300g), chopped coarsely
3 cups (750ml) vegetable stock
1½ cups (375ml) water
¼ cup (60ml) pouring cream

1 Preheat oven to 200°C/400°F.

2 Scrub artichokes. Toss artichokes in half the oil in a deep baking dish; season. Cover with foil; roast 10 minutes. Stir artichokes; roast, covered, for further 30 minutes or until tender.

3 Heat remaining oil in a large saucepan over medium heat; cook leek and celery, stirring, 10 minutes or until vegetables are caramelised. Add paste; cook, stirring, 1 minute. Stir in potato, artichokes, stock and the water; bring to the boil. Reduce heat; simmer, covered, 15 minutes or until potato is tender. Cool 10 minutes.

4 Blend soup, in batches, until smooth. Strain soup into same pan; cook, stirring, until hot. Season to taste.

5 Ladle soup into serving bowls, drizzle with cream and a little herbed butter, if you like.

nutritional count per serving 20.1g total fat (5.8g saturated fat); 1048kJ (250 cal); 12.6g carbohydrate; 3.9g protein; 3.4g fibre

notes Recipe is not suitable to freeze. Jeursalem artichokes should be hard with a knobbly, uneven surface; they have a nutty taste.

ASIAN BEEF CONSOMMÉ

prep + cook time 50 minutes **serves** 4

Heat 1 tablespoon of peanut oil in a large saucepan until it's really hot. Add 300g (9½oz) beef strips, 1 chopped red thai (serrano) chilli and 1 teaspoon grated fresh ginger; stir-fry until beef is browned. Pour in 4 cups beef consommé; bring to the boil then simmer for 30 minutes with the lid on. While the beef is cooking, soak 125g (4 ounces) bean thread vermicelli for about 5 minutes in a bowl of boiling water; drain then divide among 4 bowls. Add 1 small bunch of roughly chopped baby buk choy and 2 tablespoons of lime juice to the soup; heat until buk choy wilts then pour soup over the vermicelli.

CHINESE CHICKEN AND CORN

prep + cook time 20 minutes **serves** 4

Heat 1 teaspoon of vegetable oil in a large saucepan; cook 1 teaspoon freshly grated ginger and 2 thinly sliced green chillies for 2 minutes. Add two 505g (1lb) cans chicken and sweet corn soup, 2½ cups water and 3 cups coarsely chopped cooked chicken; bring to the boil. Reduce heat; simmer. Beat 1 egg white in a small jug with 1 tablespoon cold water then slowly pour it into the soup, stirring constantly. Serve soup sprinkled with 1 thinly sliced green onion (scallion).

note You will need a 900g (1¾lb) barbecue chicken to get the amount of meat required for this recipe.

BEEF & VEGETABLE WITH DUMPLINGS

prep + cook time 40 minutes **serves** 4

Boil or microwave 1 large chopped potato until tender; drain. Mash potato, then stir in 1 egg yolk, 3 teaspoons of chopped chives and 2 tablespoons each of flour and grated cheddar cheese until well combined. Shape tablespoons of mixture into patties; coat in ¼ cup packaged breadcrumbs. Heat about a ¼ cup of vegetable oil in a shallow frying pan; cook dumplings until browned lightly, drain well on absorbent paper. Heat two 505g (1lb) cans of beef and vegetable soup and 1 cup of water in a large saucepan until hot (do not boil). Serve bowls of soup topped with potato dumplings.

THAI CHICKEN, AND PUMPKIN

prep + cook time 30 minutes **serves** 4

Stir ¼ cup red curry paste in a large heated saucepan until fragrant. Add two 420g (13½oz) cans cream of pumpkin soup, 3¼ cups light coconut milk and 1½ cups chicken stock to pan; bring to the boil. Stir in 3 cups roughly chopped cooked chicken; reduce heat to medium, then stir until soup is heated through. Stir in 4 thinly sliced green onions (scallions) and ¼ cup roughly chopped fresh basil leaves just before serving.

note You will need a 900g (1¾lb) barbecue chicken to get the amount of meat required for this recipe.

GLOSSARY

ARTICHOKE

globe large flower-bud of a member of the thistle family; it has tough petal-like leaves, and is edible in part when cooked.

jerusalem is a tuber of a species of sunflower, and is also known as a sunchoke. Its creamy flesh has a delicious nutty taste and a crisp and crunchy texture.

BACON SLICES also known as bacon rashers.

BARLEY a nutritious grain used in soups and stews. Hulled barley, the least processed, is high in fibre.

pearl has had the husk removed and has then been steamed and polished so that only the "pearl" of the original grain remains.

BASIL an aromatic herb; there are many types, but the most commonly used is sweet, or common, basil.

thai also called horapa; different from sweet basil and holy basil in both look and taste, with smaller leaves and purplish stems. It has a slight aniseed taste.

BAY LEAVES aromatic leaves from the bay tree available fresh or dried; adds a strong, slightly peppery flavour.

BEAN SPROUTS also known as bean shoots; tender new growths of assorted beans and seeds. The most readily available are mung bean, soya bean, alfalfa and snow pea sprouts.

BEANS

black also known as turtle beans or black kidney beans; an earthy-flavoured dried bean completely different from the better-known chinese black beans (which are fermented soya beans). Used most in Mexican, South American and Caribbean cooking, especially soups and stews.

black-eyed also called black-eyed peas or cow peas. Mild-flavoured and thin-skinned, so they cook faster than most other beans.

borlotti also called roman or pink beans, can be eaten fresh or dried. Interchangeable with pinto beans due to their similar appearance – pale pink or beige with dark red streaks.

broad also known as fava, windsor and horse beans; available dried, fresh, canned and frozen. Fresh and frozen forms should be peeled twice (discarding both the outer long green pod and the beige-green tough inner shell). Are widely used in Mediterranean soups.

butter also known as lima beans; large, flat, kidney-shaped bean, off-white in colour, with a mealy texture and mild taste. Available canned and dried.

cannellini small white bean similar in appearance and flavour to great northern, navy and haricot beans – all of which can be substituted for the other. Cannellini beans are available dried and canned.

kidney medium-sized red bean, slightly floury in texture yet sweet in flavour; sold both dried and canned.

lima see butter bean.

white a generic term we use for canned or dried cannellini, navy, haricot or great northern beans – all of which can be substituted for the other.

BEEF

blade taken from the shoulder; isn't as tender as other cuts of beef, it needs slow-roasting to achieve best results.

brisket a cheaper cut from the belly; good for slow-cooking.

cheeks a very tough and lean cut of meat and is most often used for slow cooking to produce a tender result.

chuck is cut from the neck and shoulder; tends to be chewy but flavourful and inexpensive. Good for slow cooking.

gravy also known as beef shin or shank, cut from the lower shin of a cow.

shank see gravy beef.

BUK CHOY also called bok choy, pak choi, chinese white cabbage or chinese chard; has a fresh, mild mustard taste.

BUTTER use salted or unsalted butter; 125g is equal to one stick (4 ounces) of butter.

CAPSICUM also known as bell pepper or, simply, pepper. Native to Central and South America, they can be red, green, yellow, orange or purplish-black in colour. Discard the seeds and membranes before use.

CARAWAY SEEDS the small, half-moon-shaped dried seed from a member of the parsley family; adds an anise flavour.

CARDAMOM a spice native to Indian; can be purchased in pod, seed or ground form. Has a distinctive aromatic, sweetly rich flavour.

CHEESE
fetta Greek in origin; a crumbly textured goat- or sheep-milk cheese having a sharp, salty taste. Ripened and stored in salted whey.
goat made from goats' milk, has an earthy, strong taste; available in both soft and firm textures, in various shapes and sizes, sometimes rolled in ash or herbs.
gruyère a hard-rind Swiss cheese with small holes and a nutty, slightly salty flavour.
parmesan also known as parmigiano; a hard, grainy cows-milk cheese. Curd is salted in brine for a month then aged for up to 2 years.
ricotta a soft, sweet, moist, white cows-milk cheese with a slightly grainy texture.

CHICKPEAS (garbanzo beans) also called hummus or channa; an irregularly round, sandy-coloured legume. Firm texture even after cooking, a floury mouth-feel and robust nutty flavour; available canned or dried (soak for several hours in cold water before use).

CHILLI available in many types and sizes (generally the smaller the chilli, the hotter it is). Use rubber gloves when seeding and chopping fresh chillies as they can burn your skin. Removing membranes and seeds lessens the heat level.

green any unripened chilli; also some particular varieties that are ripe when green, such as jalapeño or serrano.
jalapeño pronounced hah-lah-pain-yo. Fairly hot, medium-sized, plump, dark green chilli; available pickled, canned or bottled, and fresh.
long available both fresh and dried; a generic term used for any moderately hot, long, thin chilli (about 6cm to 8cm long).
red thai also called "scuds"; small, very hot and bright red in colour.

CHINESE BARBECUED PORK roasted pork fillet with a sweet, sticky coating. Available from Asian butchers.

CHINESE COOKING WINE also known as shao hsing or chinese rice wine; made from fermented rice, wheat, sugar and salt with 13.5% alcohol. Found in Asian food shops; use mirin or sherry instead.

CINNAMON available as sticks (quills) and ground.

COCONUT
cream obtained commercially from the first pressing of the coconut flesh, without the addition of water; the second pressing (less rich) is sold as coconut milk.
milk this is not the juice found inside the fruit, which is known as coconut water, but the diluted liquid from the second pressing from the white meat of a mature coconut.

CREAM
crème fraîche mature fermented cream having a slightly tangy, nutty flavour and velvety texture. Used in savoury and sweet dishes. Minimum fat content 35%.

pouring we use pouring cream unless otherwise stated. Also known as single, fresh and pure cream; it has no additives unlike commercially thickened cream. It has a minimum fat content of 35%.
sour a thick commercially-cultured soured cream. Minimum fat content 35%.
thickened a whipping cream containing a thickener. Minimum fat content 35%.

CORIANDER also known as pak chee, cilantro or chinese parsley; bright-green leafy herb with a pungent flavour. It is one of the few fresh herbs to be sold with its root attached. It should be readily available from greengrocers. Asian greengrocers will certainly stock it. Both the stems and roots of coriander are also used in cooking. Wash the coriander under cold water, removing any dirt clinging to the roots; scrape the roots with a small flat knife to remove some of the outer fibrous skin. Chop coriander roots and stems together to obtain the amount specified. Is also available ground or as seeds; these should not be substituted for fresh coriander as the tastes are completely different.

CUCUMBER
lebanese short, slender and thin-skinned. Probably the most popular variety because of its tender, edible skin, tiny seeds, and sweet, fresh taste.
telegraph also known as the european or burpless cucumber; slender and long (35cm and more), its thin dark-green skin has shallow ridges running down its length.

CUMIN also called zeera or comino; is the dried seed of a plant related to the parsley family with a spicy, almost curry-like flavour. Available dried as seeds or ground.

CURRY PASTE some recipes in this book call for commercially prepared pastes of varying strengths and flavours. Use whichever one you feel suits your spice-level tolerance best.
green the hottest of the traditional pastes; contains hot chilli, garlic, onion, spice, lemon grass and galangal.
korma a classic North Indian paste with a rich yet mild coconut flavour with hints of garlic, ginger and coriander.
madras a hot curry paste; consisting of coriander, cumin, pepper, turmeric, chilli, garlic, ginger, vinegar and oil.
panang a sweet and milder variation of red curry paste. Contains chilli, garlic, onion, shrimp paste, lemon grass, spice and galangal.
red probably the most popular curry paste; a medium heat blend of chilli, garlic, onion, lemon grass, spice, galangal and salt.
rogan josh a paste of medium heat; made from fresh chillies or paprika, tomato and spices, especially cardamom.

CURRY POWDER a blend of ground spices used for convenience when making Indian food. Can consist of some of the following spices in varying proportions: dried chilli, cinnamon, coriander, cumin, fennel, fenugreek, mace, cardamom and turmeric. Choose mild or hot to suit your taste and the recipe.

EGGPLANT purple-skinned vegetable also known as aubergine. Can also be purchased char-grilled, packed in oil, in jars.

FENNEL also called finocchio or anise; a roundish, bulbous vegetable, about 8-12cm in diameter, with a mild licorice smell and taste. Has a large swollen base consisting of several overlapping broad stems, forming a white to very pale green-white, firm, crisp bulb. The bulb has a slightly sweet, anise flavour but the leaves have a stronger taste. Also the name given to dried seeds having a licorice flavour.

FLOUR
cornflour (cornstarch) used as a thickening agent in cooking.
plain an all-purpose flour made from wheat.
self-raising plain flour combined with baking powder in the proportion of 1 cup flour to 2 teaspoons baking powder. Also called self-rising flour.

GAI LAN also known chinese broccoli, gai larn, kanah, gai lum and chinese kale; appreciated more for its stems than its coarse leaves. Can be served steamed and stir-fried, in soups and noodle dishes.

GALANGAL also known as ka or lengkaus if fresh and laos if dried and powdered; a root, similar to ginger. It has a hot-sour ginger-citrusy flavour. Fresh ginger can be substituted.

GARAM MASALA literally means "blended spices"; based on varying proportions of cloves, cardamom, fennel, cinnamon, coriander, and cumin, roasted and ground.

GHEE a type of clarified butter used frequently in Indian cooking; milk solids are cooked until they are a golden brown (whereas in clarified butter they are not), which imparts a nutty flavour and sweet aroma; ghee can be heated to a high temperature without burning.

GINGER, FRESH also called green or root ginger; the thick gnarled root of a tropical plant. Can be kept, peeled, covered with dry sherry in a jar and refrigerated, or frozen in an airtight container.

HARISSA a Moroccan sauce or paste made from dried chillies, cumin, garlic, oil and caraway seeds. The paste, available in a tube, is very hot and should not be used in large amounts; bottled harissa sauce is more mild. From supermarkets and Middle-Eastern grocery stores.

KAFFIR LIME LEAVES also called bai magrood; looks like two glossy dark green leaves joined end to end, forming a rounded hourglass shape. Used fresh or dried, like bay leaves. Sold fresh, dried or frozen, the dried leaves are less potent so double the number if using them as a substitute for fresh; a strip of fresh lime peel may be substituted for each kaffir lime leaf.

KUMARA the Polynesian name of an orange-fleshed sweet potato often confused with yam.

LEMON GRASS also called takrai, serai or serah. A tall, clumping, lemon-smelling and tasting, sharp-edged aromatic tropical grass; the white lower part of the stem is used, finely chopped. Available from Asian food shops and greengrocers.

MUSHROOMS

button small, cultivated white mushrooms with a mild flavour. When a recipe in this book calls for an unspecified type of mushroom, use button.

enoki cultivated mushrooms; tiny, long-stemmed, pale mushrooms that grow and are sold in clusters, and can be used that way or separated by slicing off the base. They have a mild fruity flavour and are slightly crisp in texture.

oyster also known as abalone; grey-white mushroom shaped like a fan. Prized for their smooth texture and subtle, oyster-like flavour.

porcini also known as cèpes; aromatic, earthy-flavoured mushroom. *Dried porcini* is the richest-flavoured mushroom; expensive, but because they are so strongly flavoured, only a small amount is required. Must be rehydrated before use.

portobello these are mature swiss brown mushrooms. Large, dark-brown mushrooms that have a full-bodied flavour.

shiitake when fresh, are also known as chinese black or forest mushrooms; although shiitake are cultivated, they have the earthiness and taste of wild mushrooms.

shiitake, dried when dried, they are known as donko or dried chinese mushrooms; rehydrate before use.

straw named for the straw on which they are grown; are small and globe-shaped with internal stems. They are cultivated but are so fragile and deteriorate so quickly after harvesting that they are not a commercial proposition fresh, so they are usually canned.

swiss brown also known as cremini or roman, light to dark brown mushrooms with full-bodied flavour. Button or cup mushrooms can be substituted for swiss brown mushrooms.

NOODLES

fresh rice also known as ho fun, khao pun, sen yau, pho or kway tiau, depending on the country of manufacture. Can be purchased in strands of various widths or large sheets weighing about 500g, which are then cut into the desired noodle size. Chewy and pure white, they don't need pre-cooking.

ramen popular Japanese wheat noodles, sold in dried, fresh, steamed and instant forms.

rice stick also called sen lek or kway teow. They come in different widths (thin used in soups, wide in stir-fries), but all should be soaked to soften.

soba pale-brown noodle originally from Japan; made from buckwheat and varying proportions of wheat flour. Available dried and fresh.

somen is the thinnest of all the Japanese noodles (like vermicelli). It is made from organic hard wheat giving a different texture and bite. Somen is most often served cold in Japan, during the hot summer months.

udon is a thick white wheat noodle with a texture suitable for soups. Made from organic soft wheat, it is served hot or cold but is more often served hot, especially in winter. Udon is often used interchangeably with soba noodles.

NORI dried seaweed used as a flavouring, garnish or for sushi. Sold in thin sheets, plain or toasted (yaki-nori).

NUTS

HOW TO ROAST spread in a single layer on an oven tray, roast in a moderately slow oven (160°C/325°F), stirring occasionally, for 8-10 minutes, or until they're lightly golden. Be careful to avoid burning nuts.

HOW TO TOAST place shelled, peeled nuts, in a single layer, in small dry frying pan; cook, stirring constantly, over low heat, until fragrant and just changed in colour. Be careful to avoid burning nuts.

almonds can be purchased as blanched, skins removed; flaked, paper-thin slices; or as slivered, small lengthways-cut pieces.

hazelnut also known as filberts; plump, grape-size, rich, sweet nut having a brown inedible skin that is removed by rubbing heated nuts together vigorously in a tea towel.

pine also known as pignoli; not in fact a nut but a small, cream-coloured kernel from pine cones.

pistachio pale green, delicately flavoured nut inside hard off-white shells. To peel, soak shelled nuts in boiling water for about 5 minutes; drain, then pat dry with absorbent kitchen paper. Rub with cloth to remove most of the skin.

OIL

cooking spray we use a cholesterol-free cooking spray made from canola oil.

mustard is rich and full-bodied with a buttery, nutty flavour, but without the heat or strong mustard taste. Cold-pressed oil is pressed from the whole seed, with no heat treatment, and is then filtered and bottled. It has a low saturated fat content and is high in omega-3 fats.

grapeseed is a good-quality, neutral vegetable oil pressed from grape seeds. From health food stores and supermarkets.

olive made from ripened olives. Extra virgin and virgin are the best, while extra light or light refers to taste not fat levels.

peanut pressed from ground peanuts; it is the most commonly used oil in Asian cooking because of its high smoke point (capacity to handle high heat without burning).

rice bran extracted from the germ and inner husk of the rice grain; has a mild, slightly nutty, flavour.

sesame made from roasted, crushed, white sesame seeds; a flavouring rather than a cooking medium.

vegetable any of a number of oils sourced from plants rather than animal fats.

ONION

brown and white onions are interchangeable, however, white onions have a more pungent flesh.

green (scallion) also called, incorrectly, shallot; this is an immature onion picked before the bulb has formed. It has a long, bright-green edible stalk.

red also known as red spanish, spanish or bermuda onion; a sweet-flavoured, large, purple-red onion.

shallots, also called french shallots, golden shallots or eschalots; they are small, brown-skinned, elongated members of the onion family, and grow in tight clusters similar to garlic.

spring onions have crisp, narrow green-leafed tops and a round sweet white bulb larger than green onions.

OREGANO is similar to marjoram but is not as sweet and has a stronger, more pungent, flavor and aroma.

PAK CHOY similar to baby buk choy, except the stem is a very pale green, rather than white, and the top is less leafy.

PANCETTA an Italian unsmoked bacon; pork belly is cured in salt and spices then rolled into a sausage shape and dried for several weeks.

PARSLEY, FLAT-LEAF a flat-leaf variety of parsley also known as continental or italian parsley.

PASTA

macaroni tube-shaped pasta available in various sizes; made from semolina and water, and does not contain eggs.

orecchiette small disc-shaped pasta, translates literally as "little ears".

penne the Italian name of this pasta means pens, a reference to the nib-like, pointy ends of each piece of pasta. Penne comes in both smooth (lisce) or ridged (rigate) versions, and a variety of sizes.

rigatoni a form of tube-shaped pasta. It is larger than penne and is usually ridged; the end does not terminate at an angle, like penne's does.

risoni small rice-shape pasta; very similar to another small pasta, orzo, although this tends to be slightly larger.

shell this shell-shaped pasta ranges in size from tiny to extra large. Great for holding sauces and in soups.

POLENTA also called cornmeal; a flour-like cereal of dried corn (maize). Also the dish made from it.

PRESERVED LEMON RIND a North African specialty; lemons are quartered and preserved in salt and lemon juice or water. To use, remove and discard pulp, squeeze juice from rind, rinse rind well; slice according to the recipe.

PROSCIUTTO an unsmoked Italian ham; salted, air-cured and aged, prosciutto is usually eaten uncooked.

QUINOA pronounced "keen-wa". The seed of a leafy plant similar to spinach. Its cooking qualities are similar to rice; it has a delicate, slightly nutty taste and chewy texture. You can substitute rice in any dish with quinoa. It is available from most health food stores and larger supermarkets; keep quinoa sealed in a glass jar under refrigeration because it spoils easily.

SAFFRON stigma of a member of the crocus family, available ground or in strands; imparts a yellow-orange colour once infused. Quality can vary greatly; the best is the most expensive spice in the world.

SAUCE

black bean a Chinese-style sauce made from fermented soya beans, spices and flour.

chilli we use a hot variety made from thai red chillies. Use it sparingly, increasing the quantity to suit your taste.

fish also called nam pla or nuoc nam; made from pulverised salted fermented fish, most often anchovies. Has a pungent smell and strong taste, so use it sparingly.

hoisin a thick, sweet and spicy sauce made from fermented soya beans, onions and garlic.

oyster Asian in origin, this rich, brown sauce is made from oysters and their brine, cooked with salt and soy sauce, and thickened with starches. A *vegetarian mushroom oyster sauce* is also available; it is made from blended mushrooms and soy sauce.

sweet chilli a comparatively mild Thai-style sauce made from red chillies, sugar, garlic and vinegar.

Tabasco the brand name of an extremely fiery sauce made from vinegar, thai red chillies and salt. Use it sparingly.

tomato also known as ketchup or catsup; made from a blend of tomatoes, vinegar and spices

worcestershire a dark coloured condiment made from garlic, soy sauce, tamarind, onions, molasses, lime, anchovies, vinegar and other seasonings.

soy also known as sieu, is made from fermented soya beans. Several variations are available in most supermarkets and Asian food stores. We use a mild Japanese variety in our recipes; possibly the best table soy and the one to choose if you only want one variety.

dark soy is deep brown, almost black in colour with a rich, thicker consistency than other types. Pungent, though not particularly salty, it is good for marinating.

japanese soy an all-purpose low-sodium soy sauce made with more wheat content than its Chinese counterparts; fermented in barrels and aged. The best table soy and the one to choose if you only want one variety.

kecap asin a thick and salty dark soy sauce used in Malay and Indonesian cooking.

kecap manis a dark, thick sweet soy sauce used in most South-East Asian cuisines. Depending on the brand, the soy's sweetness is derived from the addition of either molasses or palm sugar when brewed.

light soy thin in consistency and, while paler than the others, is the saltiest tasting; used in dishes in which the natural colour of the ingredients is to be maintained. Not to be confused with salt-reduced or low-sodium soy sauces.

tamari a thick, dark soy sauce made mainly from soya beans without the wheat used in standard soy sauce.

SEAFOOD

blue swimmer crab also called sand crab, blue manna crab, bluey or sandy. Substitute with lobster, balmain or moreton bay bugs.

firm white fish fillet blue eye, bream, flathead, swordfish, ling, whiting, jewfish, snapper or sea perch are all good choices. Check for any small pieces of bone in the fillets and use tweezers to remove them.

prawns (shrimp) varieties include, school, king, royal red, sydney harbour, tiger. Can be bought uncooked (green) or cooked, with or without shells.

white fish means non-oily fish; this includes bream, flathead, whiting, snapper, dhufish, redfish and ling.

SILVER BEET (swiss chard) also called, incorrectly, spinach; has fleshy stalks and large leaves.

SPINACH also called english spinach and, incorrectly, silver beet. Baby spinach is also available; these tender leaves don't need to be trimmed.

STAR ANISE a dried star-shaped pod whose seeds have an astringent aniseed flavour.

SUGAR, PALM also called nam tan pip or jaggery; from the sap of the sugar palm tree. Light brown to black in colour and usually sold in rock-hard cakes; use brown sugar if unavailable.

TOFU also called soya bean curd or bean curd. Comes fresh as soft or firm, and processed as fried or pressed dried sheets. Fresh tofu can be refrigerated in water (changed daily) for up to 4 days.

TOMATO

paste triple-concentrated puree used to flavour soups.

sun-dried tomato pieces are dried with salt; this dehydrates the tomato and concentrates the flavour. We use sun-dried tomatoes packaged in oil, unless otherwise specified.

VIETNAMESE MINT not a mint at all, but a pungent and peppery narrow-leafed member of the buckwheat family; also known as cambodian mint and laksa leaf.

WOMBOK also known as napa, chinese or peking cabbage, wong bok and petsai. Elongated in shape with pale green, crinkly leaves, this is the most common cabbage in South-East Asia. Can be shredded or chopped and eaten raw or braised, steamed or stir-fried.

WONTON WRAPPERS, also known as spring roll or gow gee wrappers, are made of flour, egg and water; available in the refrigerated or freezer section of many supermarkets, and come in different thicknesses and shapes.

CONVERSION CHART

MEASURES

One Australian metric measuring cup holds approximately 250ml; one Australian metric tablespoon holds 20ml; one Australian metric teaspoon holds 5ml.

The difference between one country's measuring cups and another's is within a two- or three-teaspoon variance, and will not affect your cooking results. North America, New Zealand and the United Kingdom use a 15ml tablespoon.

All cup and spoon measurements are level. The most accurate way of measuring dry ingredients is to weigh them. When measuring liquids, use a clear glass or plastic jug with the metric markings.

The imperial measurements used in these recipes are approximate only. Measurements for cake pans are approximate only. Using same-shaped cake pans of a similar size should not affect the outcome of your baking. We measure the inside top of the cake pan to determine sizes.

We use large eggs with an average weight of 60g.

DRY MEASURES

METRIC	IMPERIAL
15g	½oz
30g	1oz
60g	2oz
90g	3oz
125g	4oz (¼lb)
155g	5oz
185g	6oz
220g	7oz
250g	8oz (½lb)
280g	9oz
315g	10oz
345g	11oz
375g	12oz (¾lb)
410g	13oz
440g	14oz
470g	15oz
500g	16oz (1lb)
750g	24oz (1½lb)
1kg	32oz (2lb)

LIQUID MEASURES

METRIC	IMPERIAL
30ml	1 fluid oz
60ml	2 fluid oz
100ml	3 fluid oz
125ml	4 fluid oz
150ml	5 fluid oz
190ml	6 fluid oz
250ml	8 fluid oz
300ml	10 fluid oz
500ml	16 fluid oz
600ml	20 fluid oz
1000ml (1 litre)	1¾ pints

LENGTH MEASURES

METRIC	IMPERIAL
3mm	⅛in
6mm	¼in
1cm	½in
2cm	¾in
2.5cm	1in
5cm	2in
6cm	2½in
8cm	3in
10cm	4in
13cm	5in
15cm	6in
18cm	7in
20cm	8in
22cm	9in
25cm	10in
28cm	11in
30cm	12in (1ft)

OVEN TEMPERATURES

The oven temperatures in this book are for conventional ovens; if you have a fan-forced oven, decrease the temperature by 10-20 degrees.

	°C (CELSIUS)	°F (FAHRENHEIT)
Very slow	120	250
Slow	150	300
Moderately slow	160	325
Moderate	180	350
Moderately hot	200	400
Hot	220	425
Very hot	240	475

INDEX

Published in 2014 by Bauer Media Books, Sydney
Bauer Media Books are published by Bauer Media Limited.

MEDIA GROUP

BAUER MEDIA BOOKS

Publisher Sally Wright
Editorial & food director Pamela Clark
Director of sales, marketing & rights Brian Cearnes
Creative director Hieu Chi Nguyen
Art director Hannah Blackmore
Designer Melissa Dumas
Senior editor Wendy Bryant
Food editor Rebecca Meli

Published and Distributed in the United Kingdom by
Octopus Publishing Group
Endeavour House
189 Shaftesbury Avenue
London WC2H 8JY
United Kingdom
phone (+44)(0)207 632 5400; fax (+44)(0)207 632 5405
info@octopus-publishing.co.uk; www.octopusbooks.co.uk

Printed in China with 1010 Printing Asia Limited.

International foreign language rights, Brian Cearnes, Bauer Media Books bcearnes@bauer-media.com.au

A catalogue record for this book is available from the British Library.

ISBN: 978 190977 012 6 (paperback)